THE BALTIC STRAITS

INTERNATIONAL STRAITS OF THE WORLD

Series Editor: Gerard Mangone,
Center for the Study of
Marine Policy
University of Delaware, U.S.A.

International Advisory Council:
Lewis Alexander, U.S.A.
Maxwell Cohen, Canada
T.B. Koh, Singapore
Ali-Moertopo, Indonesia
John R. Stevenson, U.S.A.

Also in this series:

1. Butler WE: Northeast Arctic Passage. 1978.
    ISBN 90-286-0498-7

2. Leifer M: Malacca, Singapore and Indonesia. 1978.
    ISBN 90-286-0778-1

3. Ramazani RK: The Persian Gulf and the Strait of Hormuz. 1979.
    ISBN 90-286-0069-8

4. Truver SC: The Strait of Gibraltar and the Mediterranean. 1980.
    ISBN 90-286-0709-9

5. Lapidoth-Eschelbacher R: The Red Sea and the Gulf of Aden. 1982.
    ISBN 90-247-2501-1

In preparation:

7. Park CH: The Korean Straits

INTERNATIONAL STRAITS
OF THE WORLD

The Baltic Straits

Gunnar Alexandersson

1982
MARTINUS NIJHOFF PUBLISHERS
THE HAGUE/BOSTON/LONDON

Distributors:

for the United States and Canada
Kluwer Boston, Inc.
190 Old Derby Street
Hingham, MA 02043
USA

for all other countries
Kluwer Academic Publishers Group
Distribution Center
P.O. Box 322
3300 AH Dordrecht
The Netherlands

Library of Congress Cataloging in Publication Data

Alexandersson, Gunnar.
    The Baltic Straits.

    (International straits of the world ; v. 6)
    Includes index.
    1. Skagerrak (Denmark and Norway)--International
status. 2. Kattegat (Denmark and Sweden)--International
status. 3. Sound, The (Denmark and Sweden)--Interna-
tional status. I. Title. II. Series.
JX4084.B315A38   341.4'46   81-22473
ISBN 90-247-2595-X   AACR2
ISBN 90-247-2595-x (this volume)
ISBN 90-247-2596-8 (series)

PRINTED IN THE NETHERLANDS

FOREWORD

This is the sixth book of the series of studies organized and edited at the
Center for the Study of Marine Policy at the University of Delaware on international straits of the world. From 1974 to 1982 the nations of the world have
tried to reach agreement on a comprehensive convention for the law of the sea
through the Third United Nations Law of the Sea Conference. Sessions have
been held in Caracas, Geneva, and New York attended by the representatives
of more than 150 states, and it is still uncertain when adoption of the draft
convention of 320 articles and eight annexes will take place. It is even less
certain when and whether an adequate number of states will ratify the convention, once adopted, without significant reservations, to give it legal force.

Passage through straits used for international navigation has been one of
the key sections of the draft convention on the law of the sea, with an entirely
new regime of "transit passage" incorporated in the articles. Whatever may
ultimately be adopted and ratified by states on this subject, history indicates
that several straits of the world ocean will continue to breed contention because of their strategic and economic importance to navies and trade, involving not only coastal and regional states, but also distant maritime powers.
It may be helpful, then, to review the physical characteristics, the political and
economic importance, and the legal status of certain narrows of the world
ocean, so that policy decisions by all concerned may be wisely taken in the
interests of peace, prosperity, and a sound marine environment.

For this study of the Baltic Straits, the Center was fortunate in enlisting the
talents of Gunnar Alexandersson, Professor of International Economic Geography at the Stockholm School of Economics. Born in Bergkvara, Sweden,
he has been an avid scholar of shipping and ports in the Baltic region, and a
frequent traveller through Europe, America, and Asia. He has been a research
associate at the University of Maryland and a visiting professor at both
the University of Nebraska and the University of Wisconsin. Professor
Alexandersson is the author of five books as well as co-author of *World
Shipping: Economic Geography of Ports and Seaborne Trade.*

The Baltic Straits have a long and interesting history. They were called the
Danish Straits, when Denmark was a great power that straddled those waterways and encompassed Norway, parts of Sweden, Germany, Poland, and
Estonia to the east, and also colonized the Scottish isles, the Faeroes, Iceland,
and Greenland to the west, while exercising control over much of England for
centuries. For several hundred years Denmark collected "dues" from ships
passing through the Sound and the Great Belt, the two important gateways to

the Baltic sea. In the early nineteenth century the British fleet had to force its way into the Baltic sea, denying Denmark's claim of a right to close the sea to non-littoral fleets.

Only in 1857, led by the United States, did the maritime states throw off the burden of the dues upon their commercial ships. Even then they indemnified Denmark generously, with the United States alone paying $393 million. During World War I Denmark was neutral and the straits were the object of considerable strategic attention by both Germany and Great Britain. Although mined to protect Danish neutrality, the straits were considered by London as an avenue of attack upon Germany, while the German fleet passed through the straits to meet the British fleet at Jutland on 31 May 1916. Many thousands of merchant vessels, moreover, were piloted through the minefields of the Great Belt during World War I.

During the late 1930s Denmark, like other states of Europe, came under heavy political pressure from the demands of Adolf Hitler's Third Reich in Germany, and Copenhagen was forced to sign a non-aggression pact, allow overflight of the straits, and the passage of submerged German submarines. But immediately after the defeat of Hitler, the Baltic and the straits became a political arena of potential conflict between the NATO forces of the West and the WP forces of the East, led by the Soviet Union.

Professor Alexandersson has carefully drawn the physical-hydrographic elements of the Baltic Sea and its approaches; he has vividly described the historical interests, both politically and economically of the littoral states, analyzed the legal status and uses of the Baltic Straits over time, and calculated the role of the Baltic region, with its waterways, in the global struggle between the western alliance and the Soviet bloc. He has especially delineated the delicate role of Sweden and Finland, caught between the juggernauts. Of particular value is his description of the various legal views of the Baltic Straits, particularly in light of the emerging law of the sea, and, finally, his estimate of the opportunities for peace and prosperity in this region marked for trade, environmental cooperation, and political rivalries by different systems of political economy.

The Center for the Study of Marine Policy launched this series of studies of international straits of the world with the encouragement and support of the Rockefeller Foundation, and I wish to express my deep appreciation to Elmore Jackson, Mason Willrich, and John Stremlau for their counsel and tangible assistance. At the same time I have had the benefit of observations and comments, with constructive suggestions, from a distinguished international Advisory Council including the late, esteemed Richard R. Baxter, Harvard Law School and Judge of the International Court of Justice, and the late Robert D. Hodgson, Office of the Geographer, Department of State, as well as Maxwell Cohen, formerly on the International Joint Commission (Canada-

United States), T.T.B. Koh, Permanent Representative of Singapore to the United Nations and President of the Third U.N. Law of the Sea Conference, Ali Moertopo, Center for Strategic and International Studies, Indonesia, John R. Stevenson, Sullivan and Cromwell, New York, and the late Admiral Edward Wegener, Federal Republic of Germany. To each of them I wish to express my gratitude.

All statements, judgements, or opinions within this study are the sole responsibility of the author and not to be attributed in any way to the Rockefeller Foundation, the Center for the Study of Marine Policy at the University of Delaware, or to any member of the International Advisory Council.

Gerard J. Mangone
Director

Center for the Study of Marine Policy
University of Delaware
15 March 1982

Contents

Chapter 5

Chapter 1

THE BALTIC REGION

Measured by population density or industrial capacity, the Baltic region is the northern, sparsely populated, and modestly productive periphery of the European continent. Yet throughout history the Baltic region has played a greater role in European affairs than the size of its population or their industrial output might indicate, for the region has been - and still is - a major crossroads of international trade and an area of vital strategic importance.

The Baltic region can be variously defined, depending on the purpose of the study. A treatise on water pollution would be centered on the hydrology of the region and the drainage basin of the Baltic Sea would be the natural object of study. An investigation of tourism and recreation would focus on the coast line, and a study of shipping would concentrate on Baltic ports and their hinterlands as well as their overseas relations. Here, however, political geography will be an important component of the study. After a brief description of the physical character of the region and its ecosystem, the decision-making units, the states, will be considered, leading into a detailed analysis of the Baltic Straits and their importance for international peace and economic development.

Physical Characteristics

The Baltic region located in the northwestern corner of the Eurasiatic continent, has a mild climate for its high latitude. Leningrad, Helsinki, Stockholm and Oslo are roughly on the same latitude as the southern tip of Greenland, central Hundson's Bay and the southern coast of Alaska (60°N) but their climate is not much different from that of Maine in the United States (45°N). This deviation in average annual temperature in comparison to the global mean for this range of latitudes is primarily explained by the heat transfer from lower latitudes caused by the North Atlantic Drift, a branch of the Gulf Stream, which follows the Norwegian coast to the Barents Sea. Thus, the influence of the relatively warm Atlantic Ocean is felt far inland in this region of prevailing westerly and southwesterly winds.

The anomalies of temperature are largest in the winter when isotherms in

2

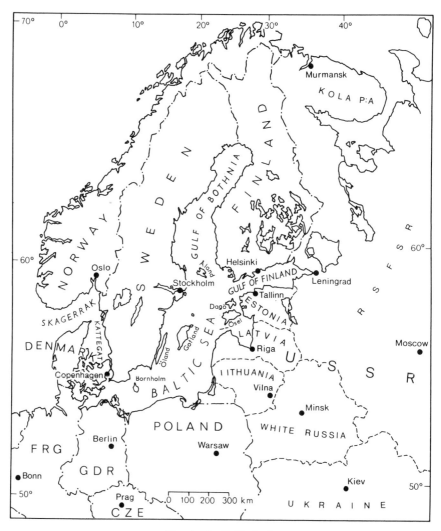

Map 1. The Baltic Region

western Europe tend to have a north-southerly direction. The isotherm for freezing (0°C) in January runs along the coast of the Scandinavian peninsula from northernmost Norway through the Sound and then south through Germany to the Alps where it turns southeastward to the Black Sea. This means that ports on the west coast of the peninsula are not much hampered by ice. Even the Kola Peninsula of the Soviet Union benefits from ice-free harbors, so that Murmansk has been an ice-free port with direct access to the world ocean, as can be seen on Map 1.

Geologically the Baltic region is both extremely old and extremely young. Large areas are composed of pre-Cambrian rocks and Quaternary glacial deposits, which means the largest stratigraphic hiatus to be found anywhere. Deposits some 15 to 20 thousand years old are found directly on top of or adjacent to rocks formed a billion years or more ago. The Fennoscandian Shield of pre-Cambrian rocks, mostly granites or gneisses, covers all of Finland and adjacent parts of the Soviet Union that can be marked by a line across the Karelian Isthmus, the Ladoga and the Onega to the White Sea and including all the Kola Peninsula. The line limiting the shield in the southeast runs under the Gulf of Finland and across the Baltic Sea north of the two Swedish islands Gotland and Öland. Southwestern Skåne and all of Denmark, except part of Bornholm, from a geological point of view belong to the continent while southern Norway is part of the shield. The Scandinavian mountains, straddling the Swedish-Norwegian border, belong to the Cambro-Silurian or Caledonian folding system. These mountains, after being worn down to a peneplain, were rejuvenated when, during the Tertiary folding of the Alps and the Carpathians, the Scandinavian Peninsula was tilted, leaving the highest points near the Norwegian Sea. Large parts of the mountains are thus made up of plateaus, such as Hardangervidda.

The latest of the four ice caps that covered the Baltic region during the Quaternary made a lasting impact on the morphology of the landscape. Most lakes were formed by natural dams deposited by the ice. Finland has been called "The Land of the Thousand Lakes", an understatement since the number of lakes in Finland and Sweden runs into many tens of thousands, the count depending on the definition of "lake". The ice sculptured the Norwegian fiords, giving them their U-form and their typical threshold at the mouth; on the Swedish side similar lakes were created. The moraine deposited by glaciers over the landscape determine which land can be cultivated and which must be left in forest. On the shield most of the arable surfaces have been under water in the post-glacial period. Their mineral soils have been restructured and organic material added. Agriculture is limited to a few percent of the land area of the shield, primarily in the coastal districts, the river valleys, and reclaimed bog or lake lands. Most of the land, which is generally covered by a thin layer of acid soil with a low humus content and very low fertility (leached podsol), supports a coniferous forest.

The massive icecap, with its central thickness of two or three thousand meters, had pressed down the land. The Scandinavian Peninsula and Finland are still in the process of bouncing back while the lands around the southern parts of the North Sea are sinking, creating special problems. The land rise is maximum west of Härnösand, Sweden and is 44 cm a century at Stockholm, with the zero-line crossing in the straits. The gain of new land around the Gulf of Bothnia has been considerable.

East, south and west of the shield, from the Gulf of Finland to Denmark, where the pre-Cambrian rocks dip under younger sediments, conditions for agriculture have always been more favorable and population densities higher. But glacial deposits also play a great role in the morphology of the landscape and in the human environment in this part of the Baltic region. The many lakes, the large end-moraines, the sandy soils, and the drainage pattern with its east-west orientation of overlarge river valleys (Urstromtäler) marking the maximum extension of the icecap are among the most conspicuous contributions of the latest ice-age to the landscape south of the Baltic. As a consequence of this orientation of the drainage pattern, East Germany, which has a coast only on the Baltic, falls almost entirely within the drainage basin of the North Sea.

Regional Trade and Transportation

Europe, with its large, enclosed seas[1] in the south and north, the Baltic, the Mediterranean, and the Black Sea, is more accessible from the ocean than other continents. No point west of the Soviet Union is more than just over 600 km from a coast. The land hemisphere - that half of the globe that holds the maximum of land (80%) and people (95%) - has northwestern Europe at its center. For centuries it has been the chief focus of world trade and world affairs. Great Britain until the First World War was the leading trading nation in the world and other nations of northwestern Europe have ranked prominently.[2]

Northwestern Europe still ranks far ahead of Anglo-America and Japan as a generator of international trade even when the intra-continental trade is disregarded.

In the early medieval period when the feudal system was at its peak in Europe and long-distance trade at its low, the Vikings had trade relations with points as far apart as Baghdad and Constantinople in the east and Greenland, Iceland, Ireland, Britain, and Spain in the west. That deeply penetrating sea in the southern periphery of Europe, the Mediterranean, which during earlier civilizations had been in the center of the known world, at this time was a battle line between Islam in North Africa and Christianity in Europe.

With the quickening of trade and the development of cities beginning in the twelfth century, the Baltic city of Lübeck played a leading economic role as the headquarters of the Hanseatic League, which included not only cities in the Baltic region but also in northern and central Germany and in the North Sea area from London to Bergen.

In the sixteenth century, as the Hansa declined, Dutch trade excelled, to be followed by British domination of trade in the eighteenth and nineteenth centuries. To the Netherlands and Britain, the Baltic region for a long period played the same role as a supplier of raw materials as their overseas colonies did later within a much larger trade volume. To both countries, the Danish-control of the straits to the Baltic Sea and the Danish-Swedish struggle for military hegemony in the Baltic region for centuries were geopolitical facts of great importance. Nevertheless, it was the initiative of the United States that brought to an end the Sound Dues in 1857, which the Danes had collected for more than four hundred years, and American action was based more on legal principle than national economic urgency.

With the Industrial Revolution the Baltic Sea and its straits lost in relative importance as a shipping region. Railroads gradually took over much of the east-west trade as Berlin, well to the south of the Baltic coast, became one of the most important railroad junctions in the world. With the construction of the Kiel Canal, moreover, an alternative was created to the Baltic Straits. Hamburg, on the North Sea, became a formidable competitor of Copenhagen for the transit trade, and in recent times Rotterdam has become a strong competitor of Gothenburg for the overseas container traffic of the Nordic countries. To both Hamburg and Rotterdam containers are hauled mainly by road and rail as well as by feeder vessels through the canal.

After the Second World War, coastal liner shipping all but disappeared in northwestern Europe, and the railroads have also been losing their relative importance to the roads. General cargo, shipped in unit loads and hauled by trucks or trains, tend to follow the shortest route from origin to destination. Roll-on, roll-off ferries act as bridges across the Baltic Straits or between points in the Nordic countries and points on the Continent for these type of transports and for passenger cars. Much of the international passenger traffic and some cargo have been taken over by airplanes. For passengers and general cargo, transportation by ship no longer is an attractive alternative.[3]

The Baltic and the straits act as barriers to the new modes of transportation, making them slower and more expensive. Cross traffic has become as important as through traffic in the straits. Skåne, the southern tip of Sweden, acts as a bridgehead for most of the ferry traffic that connects the road and railway nets of Finland, Sweden, and Norway with those of the continent. The large flows passing over Denmark require two ferry passages between the continent and the Scandinavian Peninsula, and those with origin or destination in Finland require three, if they do not move directly by roll-on, roll-off ferry between Helsinki and Travemünde, as shown in Map 2. For the international ferry traffic in the terminals on the map, see Table 1.

For bulk cargo, sea transport is still the cheapest means so that ports are the most competitive location for heavy industry and bulk storage. Since bulk cargo completely dominates international trade by weight, the flow of cargo in the Baltic Sea and through the straits and the Kiel Canal have been larger than

6

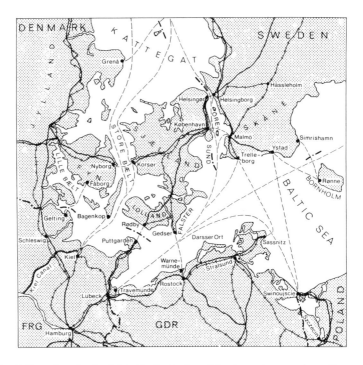

Map 2. Ferry lines in the Baltic Straits Region. Inland are shown major railways and Europe-roads. The Malmö - Karlskrona - Norrköping road (E66) was reclassified after the map was completed.

ever in spite of the almost complete loss of general cargo and passenger traffic to other modes of transportation. Even though the cargo and passenger flows no longer follow their old patterns through the straits or the canal, but rather use ferries or airplanes, the small Helsingborg-Malmö-Lübeck-Kiel-Nyborg-Helsingborg area remains the crossroads for traffic to and from the Baltic region. Copenhagen is the undisputed air gateway to the Nordic countries and one of the largest airports in Europe. It is also the rail gateway, now operating chiefly through the rail-ferry at Helsingør-Helsingborg. Ferries serving road traffic have tried to avoid metropolitan cities and tend to be scattered in both their Scandinavian and their continental terminals. For example, several ferry lines from Norway and the west coast of Sweden have their continental terminals on the Jutland Peninsula, which lies outside the Baltic region.

Table 1

Ferry Traffic at Baltic Terminals Covered by Map 2
(weekly connections)

Terminal	Frequency	Terminal	Frequency	Terminal	Frequency
Gelting	14-21	Rønne	7-40	Göteborg	11
Kiel	21-34	Ystad	21-49	Oslo	4-6
Puttgarden	Frequent*	Trelleborg	56	Helsingør	Frequent
Travemünde (Incl Lübeck)	75-79	Malmö (Incl Limhamn and Landskrona)	14 Frequent	Copenhagen (Incl Dragør)	15-17 Frequent
Warnemünde	21-28			Gedser	21-28
Sassnitz	35	Helsingborg	14 Frequent	Rødby	Frequent
Swinoujscie	20	Varberg	14-28	Korsør	4-7
Helsinki	17-24			Bagenkop	10-21
Simrishamn	0-5			Fåborg	14-21
				Grenå	14-28

* Sailings every hour or so over short distances.

Chapter 2

THE BALTIC SEA AS AN ECOSYSTEM

The world ocean has been conveniently divided by oceanographers along arbitrarily chosen lines.[1] Several "adjacent seas" of the North Atlantic Ocean have been distinguished: namely, the Caribbean Sea, the Gulf of Mexico, the Mediterranean Sea, the Black Sea, the Polar Seas, Baffin Bay, the Labrador Sea, the Norwegian Sea and the Baltic Sea. The limit of the Baltic area is normally drawn either just north of the straits or on the latitude of the Skagen (Skaw), which means that the Kattegat sometimes is included. However, the Skagerack has never been regarded as part of the Baltic area, and Norway is not considered a littoral state of the Baltic.[2]

In the Gdańsk Fishing Convention (Convention on Fishing and Conservation of the Living Resources in the Baltic Sea and the Belts, signed in Gdańsk on 13 September 1973 and ratified on 28 July 1974), which established a commission for cooperation in fishing matters between the seven littoral states of the Baltic, headquartered in Warsaw, the line was drawn just north of the Belts from Hasenøre Head south of Aebeltoft on Jutland to Gniben Point, Korshage, Spodsbjerg and Gilbjerg Head, all on Sjaelland, and to Kullen in Sweden. Kattegat was not included. The London Fishing Conventions of 1946 and 1973, regulating the meshes of fishing nets and the size limits of fish, the Paris Convention of 1974, regulating marine pollution from landbased sources and the Copenhagen Agreement of 1974 between Denmark and Sweden, regulating pollution in the Sound, use the same limit.

Part IX of the Draft Convention (Informal Text) on the Law of the Sea, which was elaborated by the Third UN Conference on the Law of the Sea from 1974 to 1980, defined an "enclosed or semi-enclosed sea" as "a gulf, basin or sea surrounded by two or more states". One or both of the following two qualifications must also be filled: the sea must be "connected to the open seas by a narrow outlet" or consist "entirely or primarily of the territorial sea and exclusive economic zones of two or more coastal states".[3] The Baltic Sea, like the Black Sea and the Mediterranean Sea, fits both qualifications, but the North Sea meets only the second. The North Sea has two outlets to the high sea and the northern outlet is far from narrow. Moreover, as a descriptive term, "enclosed sea" for the three European seas may be acceptable, but as a legal concept it seems highly controversial.

Map 3. Drainage basin and subregions of the Baltic Sea and its transition area.
A) Baltic proper: 1 Oder (Odra), 2 Vistula (Wisla, Weichsel), 3 Pregel (Pregolja), 4 Neman (Nemunas, Memel), 25) North & South River (Norrström, Söderström), 26 Motala River (Motala ström)
B) Bothnian Sea: 11 Kokemäen River or joki, 19 Ume River or älv, 20 Ångerman River Ångermanälven), 21 Indal River (Indalsälven), 22 Ljungan, 23 Ljusnan, 24 Dal River Dalälven),
C) Bothnian Bay: 12 Oulu River or joki, 13 Kemi River or joki, 14 Torne River or älv, 15 Kalix River or älv, 16 Lule River or älv, 17 Pite River or älv, 18 Skellefte River or älv,
D) Gulf of Finland: 6 Narva, 7 Luga, 8 Neva, 9 Saima Canal, 10 Kymi River or joki,
E) Gulf of Riga: 5 Dvina (Daugava, Düna), F) Belt Sea, G) Kattegat: 27 Göta River or älv.

The North Sea has been often considered as part of the North Atlantic Ocean. From a geographic and historic point of view, the North Sea and the Baltic Sea are separate entities and both differ from the North Atlantic Ocean proper.[4] The rather narrow Norwegian Deep, which stretches far into Skagerack south of the Norwegian coast, is the only large area below the 200-meter isobath and has a maximum depth of 690 meters. But in a global oceanographic context, considering salt water, tides and so forth, the North Sea is a part of the North Atlantic Ocean rather than related to the Baltic Sea and historically the two have always been regarded as separate units. Map 3 shows the drainage of the Baltic Sea.

Depths

The Baltic Sea (including the Belt Sea and the Sound) is shallow with a mean depth of 54 meters, a surface of 393,000 km^2 and a volume of 21,200 km^3. It is the world's largest area of brackish water. The Baltic proper (200,000 km^2) is separated from the straits in the south-west by sills, at the southern Sound (eight meters) and the Darss Threshold (12 to 14 meters) through which there are somewhat deeper sailing channels. The Baltic proper can be divided into three basins separated by thresholds or extended areas of more shallow water, as shown in Map 4. Between Skåne and Rügen lies the Arkona Basin with a maximum depth of 55 meters, which has a threshold of 46 meters between Bornholm and Skåne. Stretching from the Hanö Bay in the direction of Poland is the Bornholm Basin (106 meters), which has a 60-meter threshold (the Stolpe Channel) leading to the large Central Basin, which is subdivided into separate basins: The Gdańsk Basin (113 meters), the East Gotland Basin (249 meters) and the West Gotland Basin (192 meters). The Landsort Deep south of Stockholm (459 meters) is a narrow rift valley, just two to three kilometers wide. It is the deepest place in the Baltic. The Åland Sea in the north separates the Baltic proper from the Bothnian Sea and the Bothnian Bay, together referred to as the Gulf of Bothnia. The Åland Sea has a maximum depth of 285 meters, the Bothnian Sea 293 meters and the Bothnian Bay 126 meters. The threshold depths between the Baltic proper and the Åland Sea range from 45 to 70 meters; between the Åland Sea and the Bothnian Sea, 90 meters; and between the latter and the Bothnian Bay (North Quarken), 25 meters. The Gulf of Finland and the Gulf of Riga are also separate parts, as shown in Map 4.

The rapid increase in size and draft of vessels after the mid-1950s made new sea charts imperative for the shallow waters of the North Sea and the Baltic, which has long been a nodal region of world trade, and has a high density of shipwrecks that add to the hazards of shipping. In the brackish water of the

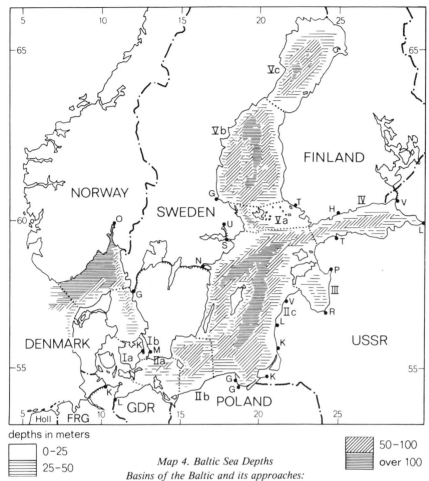

Map 4. Baltic Sea Depths

depths in meters
0–25
25–50
50–100
over 100

Basins of the Baltic and its approaches:
The Belt Sea (Ia), the Sound (Ib), the Arkona Basin (IIa), the Bornholm Basin (IIb),
the Central Basin (IIc), the Gulf of Riga (III), the Gulf of Finland (IV), the Åland Sea (Va),
the Bothnian Sea (Vb) and the Bothnian Bay (Vc).
The latter two (Vb + c) are referred to as the Gulf of Bothnia.

Baltic the ship worm does not occur so that wooden hulls have been preserved for hundreds of years at the bottom of the sea. The best known example is the *Vasa*, which went down in 1628 and was lifted in 1961. New techniques for depth measurements have been developed, partly as a result of the demand for new charts, but to save on expensive measurements of vast areas, special corridors for large vessels were charted to the major Baltic ports joining the T-route through the Baltic approaches.[5]

Morphology

The Baltic seabed is part of the continental shelf, only a small part lying in water deeper than 200 meters.[6] The morphology of the Baltic bottom and of surrounding land areas has been strongly modified by the work of the icecap that during the latest ice age covered the Nordic countries - except for the western rim of the Jutland Peninsula - nearby parts of the Soviet Union, Poland (just north of Warsaw), and Germany (just south of Berlin).

The postglacial sea started to form some 14,000 years ago with the melting of the icecap and the successive northward recession of the ice rim. The form, the outlets, and the salinity of the Baltic shifted considerably in this period, which was short in geologic time. The Baltic Ice Lake was formed between the ice rim in the north - marked by pronounced moraines such as Salpausselkä of southern Finland, the central Swedish moraines south of Stockholm, the raes of southern Norway, and the mainland in the south. However, some 9,500 years ago a sound was opened north of Mount Billingen in Sweden and the Baltic became a gulf of the ocean, the Yoldia Sea. A millenium later the icecap had melted. Southern Sweden was still connected with the Continent, and Great Britain was linked by a land bridge to Denmark. The land rise in central Sweden changed the archipelago into terra firma and the Baltic into a lake, Lake Ancylus. Vast areas north and south of Lake Mälaren and Lake Hjälmaren in east-central Sweden were under water and the Gulf of Bothnia was much wider than now. Most of Finland was actually sea bottom. With a continued rapid rise of the land in the north and a slow sinking in the south the Belts and the Sound came into existence some 6,500 years ago, forming the Litorina Sea.

According to the classical development scheme for the postglacial Baltic Sea, the Baltic has changed twice from a lake to a gulf of the sea, and has been named for mollusks or mussels typical of the respective period. The Baltic is now something in-between, neither a sea nor a lake, but an area of brackish water. Its short development period and its brackish, cold water make the Baltic biologically very sensitive. The recent or Quaternary geologic history of the Baltic region, both on-shore and off-shore, is helpful for an understanding not only of the landforms and drainage patterns but of the whole ecosystem.

With its shallow entrance the Baltic Sea is often compared with a fiord. The Kattegat has an average depth of only 23 meters and a threshold depth in the deepest channel near the Swedish coast of 20 meters. As noted earlier, the threshold depth in the southern end of the Sound is eight meters and the Darss Threshold between Gedser on Falster and Darss Ort on the German mainland is 12 to 14 meters. The Kadet sailing channel through this ridge, which separates the Arkona Basin and the Bay of Mecklenburg, has a controlling depth of 17 meters. It is eight nautical miles away from the coast of the German Democratic Republic (GDR).

The southern sills limit the exchange of water between the Baltic and the ocean. They are covered by sand and some gravel, which are the major concrete aggregates and road-building materials used by the construction industry of northern Europe. A deepening of the sills would not only be feesible but might also become profitable. However, it would have a significant impact on the hydrology of the Baltic, not only on temperature and salinity but also on the biochemical conditions as well, and any such deepening would require consultation with all the littoral states. The consequences could be helpful to the ecosystem. Higher water temperature, more salinity, and shorter flushing periods could make deepening by sand excavation or the blasting of limestone bottoms attractive to all parties concerned. The old Litorina Sea was twice as salty as the present Baltic Sea and its sediments do not show the signs of a stagnant or semi-stagnant milieu that recently has caused so much alarm among Baltic scholars studying sulfide-containing clays and muds. But more research and base data will be needed for safe predictions of the hydrological consequences of deepening the sills. A significant deepening of the sills would also be of importance to shipping and have strategic consequences for naval planning.

In international relations the deepening of the sills in the Sound and at Darss would pose unique problems. Assuming a 12-mile territorial sea, the sills would fall within the jurisdiction of the two strait states, but the dredging would have consequences for both the high seas in the Baltic and the territorial waters as well. Dredging in international straits would be in the interest of world shipping. Since the approaches of the Baltic do not connect two parts of the ocean, but rather the ocean with an enclosed sea of brackish water, dredging will not only affect shipping, but the whole ecosystem.[7] With a 200-mile economic zone the management of this ecosystem would be the responsibility of the littoral states.

The planned construction of bridges across the Sound and the Belts has been opposed by the states of the Eastern bloc and they have suggested that the text of a convention contain the following passage: "The coastal State shall not place in the straits any installations which could interfere with or hinder the transit of ships".[8] By accomodating the tallest ships in existence the bridge builders could meet this requirement. However, in a conflict involving a straits state, the destruction of the bridge could temporarily reduce the available depth for ships carrying cargo as well as for navy vessels going in and out of the Baltic. It should be possible to define "temporarily" in terms of hours or days, and in the Baltic approaches most ships sailing in and out of Baltic ports can use alternative routes. Thus, they would not be affected by the reduced depth under one bridge, unless it could be shown that a reduced depth, caused by the collapse of a bridge, would be less than the threshold depth of their only available route.

Advanced plans for international bridges across the Sound at Copenhagen-Malmö and at Helsingborg-Helsingør have been postponed for financial reasons; the construction of a domestic bridge across the Great Belt between Korsør and Nyborg has also been delayed. An international bridge between Rødby an Puttgarden lies much further in the future.

Geology

In spite of its shallow water and its proximity to several academic research centers, the bottom of the Baltic Sea has not been well known geologically until new techniques in the late 1950s made it possible to assemble and analyze data on a large scale. A very important research tool was the continuously registering reflection seismograph, similar to the echo-sounder in its operation, which provided a continuous profile of the bottom. Profiles of the Baltic floor are often harder to obtain and interpret than profiles of much deeper ocean floors due to seismically "difficult" sediments, glacial deposits of varying thickness, and so forth.[9] So far no detailed geologic map has been published of the Baltic Sea floor, but Map 5 provides a general view.

The pre-Cambrian Shield that makes up almost all of Finland and most of Sweden north of southwestern Skåne dips under Cambrian and later sediments in the Baltic Sea. The oldest sediments follow a wide arc from the Kalmar Sound to the Gulf of Finland and the Ladoga. Successively younger sediments have been added, marked by cuestas. The Ordovician cuesta, a conspicuous landscape feature along the west coast of Öland, can be traced among the isobaths to northern Estonia, where the Glint rises as high as 150 meters above the narrow terrace that skirts the gulf. Its eroded remnants form hundreds of islands along the coast of Estonia. The Silurian cuesta follows a more or less parallel course from northwestern Gotland to Estonia. The Devonian cuesta follows halfway between Gotland and Ventspils. For a petroleum geologist the Baltic floor is very unpromising, except for areas close to the Soviet, Polish, and German coasts; very little oil and natural gas in the world have been found in Cambro-Silurian deposits. However, the younger sediments of the souteastern and southern Baltic cut across the southwestern corner of Skåne, Sweden, and they form all of Denmark as well as the petroleum-rich floor of the North Sea.

Hydrology

The basic reason for the brackish water of the Baltic is that preciptitation dominates evaporation in its drainage basin. The other large enclosed sea of

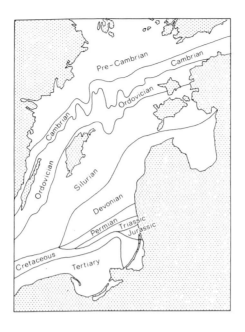

Map 5. Baltic Sea Floor Geology (Map adapted after V Gudelis, Vilnius, 1970)

Europe, the Mediterranean, has somewhat supersalt water because evaporation exceeds precipitation in that dry part of the world. The brackish water body of the Baltic, which makes it unique among the seas, is maintained by the inflow of salt water from the ocean in the south and of river water from all sides, especially in the north.[10] The annual outflow has been estimated to be twice the inflow, 940 km³ versus 470 km³. Annual precipitation over the water body roughly equals evaporation. This creates a horizontal surface gradient of eight parts per thousand over a distance of 1,500 km, from 10 parts per thousand in the southern part of the Sound to almost fresh water, two parts per thousand in the extreme north.[11] Along the Swedish west coast of 300 km, salinity increases to 30 parts per thousand or almost ocean water. The fresh water supply to the Baltic has been estimated at 15,000 cubic meters per second or 470 km³ per year, which is 2.2% of its volume. Due to the Coriolis force, produced by the rotation of the earth, the isohalines are oriented southwest-northeast. This is in accordance with Ferrel's Law, which states that objects, fluids, or gases in the northern hemisphere deviate to the right from their path of motion.

A surface stream of relatively low salinity follows the Swedish coast and moves through the Sound and along the Swedish west coast where it is known as the Baltic Stream. Its charactaristic speed is 10 centimeters per second.

When the water is ice-covered, the current slows down to a few centimeters per second. A branch of the Jutland Stream moves in the opposite direction and carries relatively salt water through the Great Belt and along the coasts of Germany, Poland, and Balticum towards the north.

The presence of sills at the narrow entrances of the Baltic leads to a sharp vertical stratification of the water body. The difference in density between the inflowing saltier water following the bottom and the outflowing fresher water in the surface stream actually creates two vertically separate water bodies. The contact zone between the two water bodies, the halocline, is at a depth of 30 meters in the Arkona Basin between Rügen and Skåne, at 40 meters in the Bornholm Basin east of Bornholm, and at 60 meters in the Central Basin at Gotland, where it separates surface water of seven parts per thousand and bottom water of 13 parts per thousand. It acts as an efficient lid, preventing a vertical water exchange. In the beginning of the century the halocline at Gotland was at a depth of 80 meters. In the Gulf of Bothnia, the halocline is much less pronounced, only one part per thousand in the far north, which means that this area has the best vertical circulation of water in the Baltic Sea. South of the sill at the Åland Islands, a strong halocline is everywhere in evidence, which makes the Baltic different from the ocean. Thus, the shallow Baltic Sea, partly because of its halocline, has posed greater problems for scientific depth measurement than the deep world ocean, and can provide some better hiding places for submarines than the much deeper ocean water.

The inflow of salt and oxidized bottom water is influenced by wind conditions over the North Atlantic. Persistent westerly winds may press salt water through the Baltic straits, building up to pulses that proceed from basin to basin. Winds from the southwest to the northwest may create southmoving surface flows in the straits of up to four knots. The whole water pillar then moves south into the Baltic. Conversely, strong winds from the southeast to the south create a north-moving surface flow of up to five knots. Normally the straits have Baltic surface water flowing north and Kattegat bottom water flowing south. However, the small in- and outflows in relation to the total volume of the Baltic makes the average turnover time of the water very long, some 25-40 years.

The Baltic has no noticeable tide. High and low water are irregular since they are caused by shifts in wind direction. Easterly winds blow water out of the Baltic and westerly winds lead to high water. Deviations of 80 centimeters or more from the normal water level are exceedingly rare.

The Baltic is a cold sea. Ice is a serious navigational hazard in the Baltic, which is not the case in the same latitudes of the Norwegian Sea, for the North Atlantic Drift creates anomalies for temperature and ice. The brackish water contributes to the serious ice problems in the Baltic. Finland is the most completely ice-blocked country in the world. The Finns have made a living out of solving this problem for themselves and other high-latitude countries by building icebreakers for the world market, including the Soviet Union. The Finnish Shipping Board has published excellent maps of the ice situation in the Baltic and its approaches.[12] Winters have been classified as severe when more than 200 of the 420 thousand square kilometers of the Baltic and its approaches (to the Skaw-Grimstad line) are frozen. Starting with 1830, eleven years have been extremely cold, which means that the whole surface has been frozen. Eight such ice winters occured before the turn of the century. The latest was in 1947, preceded by the classical "war" winters of 1940-42. Two years, 1940 and 1942, belonged to this category, and 1941 "almost" belonged. The only decade since 1830 without any winter in the severe category was 1930-1939.

In a normal winter from 100 to 200 thousand square kilometers are frozen. The "southward" line demarcating ice during a normal winter follows the Swedish coast from the northern tip of Öland to the Åland Sea and then turns south off Dagö (Hiiumaa), Ösel (Saaremaa) and the Latvian coast. The "northward" limit closely follows the Swedish coast from Roslagen north of Stockholm to North Quarken and then close to the Finnish coast into the Gulf of Finland to just east of Helsinki and then close to the Estonian coast to Dagö. Light winters are about as frequent as severe ones and somewhat more frequent this century than last.

Since about 1970 Finnish ports have been kept open even in the far north (Kemi, Oulu and Raahe). In the east, Kotka and, with few exceptions, Hamina were kept open at least ten years earlier. Of the eight icebreakers in service along the coasts of Finland, the two largest, *Urho* and *Sisu*[13] have 22.000 horsepower motors. To follow the icebreakers through the Baltic ice in winter, ships must be of a certain size and classified for movement in ice. Ships are continuously informed about the ice situation through the weather reports on the radio. On the Swedish side of the Gulf of Bothnia shipping operates with the help of icebreakers just as in Finland.

Biology

Aqueous life depends on the availability of dissolved nitrogen and phosphorous. Too much nutrition leads to an excessive growth of phytoplankton, which are at the beginning of the food chain. This process, eutrophication, was first noted in lakes and in the brackish water of the Baltic Sea.

The ocean holds a wide spectrum of plants and animals and so do fresh water lakes, but the mixing zone between the two is extremely poor in species. Few species from either habitat have been able to adapt themselves to diluted sea water. The poorest water environment can be found in the salinity interval between four and eight parts per thousand, which includes most of the Baltic Sea. Thus, while on the Swedish west coast more than 1,200 macroscopic species are known, the corresponding number for the Åland Sea - the open water between the Stockholm and the Åland archipelagoes -is only a little more than 50. In addition, the salt water species are likely to appear dwarfed in the brackish water of the Baltic. The best known example is the herring which, when landed at Kalmar and places further to the north, is known as *strömming*. From Stockholm and northwards, it is of the size of a sardine. Another example is the blue mussel which on the west coast is ten centimeters but in the Baltic only three centimeters. In the Baltic this mussel avoids the surface water, which often may be further diluted by rain, but even at a depth of five to ten meters it does not obtain sufficient nutrition for normal growth.[14]

The natural contents of phosphorous and nitrogen in the surface water of the Baltic are fairly small. The source of additional phosphate is mainly sewage, particularly detergents and human waste. Organic particles from the surface are metabolized by using the dissolved oxygen of the water on their way down. In contrast to the well-mixed surface layer, the bottom water has low and often critical oxygen values due to the consumption of oxygen by bottom bacteria. When all the oxygen has been used up, the environment switches to an anaerobic state, hostile to higher forms of life. This environment is dominated by sulfur bacteria and hydrogen sulfide producers. The bottom sediments turn from semi-stagnant to stagnant. The Baltic thus is different from the ocean, which never lacks oxygen, even at the greatest depths, and vertical and horizontal sea currents provide the oxygen necessary for higher forms of life.

Pollution

Stratification of the water, long turnover time, and low temperatures make the Baltic Sea sensitive to an increased load of nutrients. Stagnant zones have narrowed or widened intermittently with the inflow of North Sea water, and stagnation periods in the Baltic have occured many times in recent centuries. But this does not exclude the likelihood that man may have contributed to an increase in the frequency of anaerobic periods. Available data indicate that the oxygen content of the bottom water in the Baltic has decreased in this century while the hydrogen sulfide of the bottom sediments has increased. However, it has not been possible to establish a causal relation between this development and the contemporary increase in water pollution.

In the 1960s the oxygen conditions of the deep basins in the Baltic attracted world-wide attention. Several littoral states organized research projects. Since low temperature and brackish water obviously made the Baltic Sea an area of precarious biological balance, it was possible to reach political consensus about the need for sewage cleaning plants. In the 1970s Sweden radically cleaned the municipal sewage dumped into the Baltic from its long coast. Other littoral countries also started to build such cleaning installations, prodded by the 1974 Helsinki Convention, although it was not ratified by all signatory states until 1980. No longer is crude sludge piped into the sea, but rather a diluted, relatively clean mixture enters the water. This has greatly improved the coastal environment, so that in central Stockholm politicians have swum in front of TV-cameras at waterfronts that were off the list of public beaches for decades while in the same waters salmon and other attractive fish can now be caught by sport fishermen.

Whether these developments have had any effect on the stagnant environment of the deeps in the Baltic is more controversial. The deeps seem to be rejuvenated by the irregular pulses of salty and oxidized water from the ocean caused more or less by the meteorological situation in the North Atlantic region.

The alarm clock that awakened the public to man's negative impact on the ecosystem of the Baltic was the observation of increased concentrations of chlorinated hydrocarbons in fish and birds. Such substances as DDT and PCB are extremely resistant to degradation. Ingested by animals, DDT is stored in the fatty parts of the animal and transmitted up the food chain with increasing concentration. The high concentration in certain birds has led to deterioration of their eggshells and eventually to sterility, which endangered the survival of the species. Heavy metals, such as mercury, cadmium, and silver, also ingested by fish or birds, are harmful in concentration.

A comparison of North Sea and Baltic fish and bird populations of the same species showed up to ten times higher concentrations of harmful substances in the Baltic Sea population. Carnivores, such as the heron and the white tailed eagle, had up to 100 times the concentration of harmful substances of the same species in the North Sea. Early DDT and mercury bans in Sweden have had remarkably positive results. The guillemots — narrow-billed, diving birds — in the middle of the Baltic, who used to be heavily polluted, by 1980 had mercury concentrations down to their 19th century level, and there are clear indications that the eagle, seriously endangered, will survive along the Swedish east coast.

The Baltic Sea has served as a testing area for regional cooperation in pollution abatement. The Swedish government convened the maritime authorities of the Baltic states at Visby in 1969 and 1970 for preliminary discussions that eventually led to the signing of the Helsinki Convention in 1974 (Convention for the Protection of the Marine Environment of the Baltic Sea Area), which has placed great responsibility on the contracting states for reducing pollution. If successful, the Baltic environmental policies may serve as a model for the rest of the world.

To make it possible for ship captains to comply with the strict regulations of the Helsinki Convention, implemented by the laws of the individual coastal states,[15] ports must supply facilities for the collection of garbage and toilet refuse as well as oil and dirty water from the cleaning of oil tanks. The convention comes close to making it an offense to throw anything overboard from a ship. Tankers and other vessels have been watched more carefully for oil spills and other violations of the rules laid down in the convention. The capacity for meeting an emergency in connection with the grounding of tankers is also being improved, for oil spills are serious threats not only to recreation interests but also to bird and fish life in the archipelagoes and along the coasts of the Baltic. The planes and boats of the coast guards have been gradually obtaining more sophisticated instruments for detecting oil spills at night and in rainy or foggy weather. Finally, to reduce oil pollution, the Baltic coastal states signed an agreement in May 1980 by which oil tankers of 20,000 gross tons or more and gas and chemical tankers of 1,600 gross tons or more will have to report their position, load, and route on entering or leaving the Baltic. The system entered into effect on 1 January 1981 and will last for a two year test period.

Fisheries

Although the Baltic fish catches doubled in ten years from 1965 to 1975 to a total annual catch of 960,000 tons, the brackish water in the Baltic is still nutrient-poor compared to the salt water in the adjacent North Sea fishing areas. As "overfishing" became an acute problem in the North Sea and the littoral states claimed wider fishing zones, fishermen from Baltic countries were partly squeezed out of their old fishing grounds in the North Sea. For instance, Sweden's west coast fleet of trawlers, which usually sailed to the North Sea, in recent years have increasingly operated in the Baltic out of ports on the south-east coast. The vessels are larger and more modern than those of the local fishermen.

The specter of depletion of fish in the Baltic Sea led to cooperation among the littoral states, and in 1975 they formed the Baltic Sea Fisheries Commission with headquarters in Warsaw. Under the influence of the UN Law of the Sea Conference negotiations from 1974 to 1982, the Baltic states have been dividing their sea into national fishing zones of exclusive jurisdiction, supplemented with bilateral agreements for fishing quotas in each other's zones.

Three species, herring, sprat, and cod, account for 90 percent of the catch, as shown in Table 2. Salmon and eel are important because of their high value as "luxury" foods. The "salty", southern parts of the Baltic provide the largest total catches of the five species shown in Table 2, especially cod, salmon, and eel.

Table 2

Baltic Fish Catches: Tonnage and Species, 1975
(Thousand tons)

Country	Herring	Sprat	Cod	Salmon	Eel	Total
USSR	113.7	114.6	49.3	0.2	-	277.8
Poland	68.5	62.4	69.3	0.0	-	200.2
GDR	71.7	11.8	14.7	0.0	-	98.2
Denmark	18.3	9.1	62.5	1.2	2.1	93.2
Sweden	60.6	2.6	18.0	0.8	1.1	83.1
Finland	65.5	6.9	0.3	0.7	-	73.4
FRG	10.5	0.9	22.0	0.1	0.1	33.6
Total	408.8	208.3	236.1	3.0	3.3	859.5

Sources: Baltic Fisheries Commission, *Proceedings of the Third Session,* Warsaw, 1977.
Baltic Salmon Working Group, *Reports on Baltic Salmon and Sea Trout,* 1977.
Denmarks Fiskeri - og Havundersøgelser, *Fiskeri og Fiskbestande,* June 1977.

Poland and the German Democratic Republic, like Finland, have coasts on-ly on the Baltic, but in contrast to Finland most of their catches are taken else-where, as suggested by Table 3. Both countries have long-term strategies for utilizing the world ocean more fully. They have fleets of large fishing vessels that can economically participate in the activity on distant fishing grounds, and they are interested in unimpeded passage through the Baltic approaches for their deep-sea fishing vessels and supply ships.

Seabed Delimitation and Mineral Production

Article 6 of the 1958 Geneva Convention on the Continental Shelf had pro-vided guidelines for the delimitation of the continental shelf for states whose coasts were opposite or adjacent to each other. States were to determine their boundaries by agreement, but in the absence of agreement, unless there were "special circumstances", the boundary would be the median line between them, that is, a line from which every point was equidistant from the nearest point of the baselines from which the territorial sea of a state is measured. In the *North Sea Continental Shelf Cases* in 1969 between Germany and Den-mark and the Netherlands, the International Court of Justice decided that the

Table 3

Baltic Fish Catches: Shares by Baltic States, 1975

Country	Quantity (percent)	Value (percent)
Finland	100	100
Denmark	6	20
Poland	33	40
Sweden	45	55
GDR	34	40
USSR	3	5
FRG	6	10

Source: Sikkerhedspolitisk studiegrupp, *Østersøen* (Copenhagen: Schultz, 1979), p. 115
      Values partly estimated for Denmark, Sweden, and Finland.

median line was not an absolute rule, especially for states that had not ratified the Convention on the Continental Shelf, and that "equitable principles" could be taken into consideration in the delimitation of a continental shelf boundary between states.

In the Baltic Sea the seven coastal states (Finland, the Soviet Union, Poland, the German Democratic Republic, the Federal Republic of Germany, Denmark, and Sweden) started to sign bilateral agreements in 1965.[16] But some, especially those between the Soviet Union and Sweden and between Poland and Denmark, ran into difficulties.[17] Sweden has maintained that its baseline for measurement of the continental shelf boundary is the island of Gotland while the Soviet Union wants to draw the boundary line midway between the two mainlands. Denmark has held the same view in its negotiations with Poland and wants to use the island of Bornholm as its baseline while Poland only accepts a territorial sea around Bornholm. Ironically, the outstanding difference between Denmark and Sweden in dividing the continental shelf between them is that Denmark wants to use three small islands in the Kattegat (Laesø, Anholt, and Hesselø) for its baseline while Sweden considers these islands too small and wants the line midway between Jutland and Halland.

The exploitation of seabed resources in the Baltic Sea is still in its infancy. The shallowness of the Baltic would make it very attractive for oil and gas prospecting were it not for its unpromising geological formations. The northern half of the seabed is pre-Cambrian and can therefore be ruled out for hydrocarbon resources. The only exception is an area of limestone deposits in the Bothnian Sea, but these are Cambro-Silurian and for that reason alone appear to be a poor risk for oil prospectors since only one or two percent of world production originates in such old formations. In the central basin of the Baltic, all territory on the Swedish side - wherever the midline will eventually be drawn - is Cambro-Silurian. In spite of this a consortium of private and state interests in the Oljeprospekterings AB (OPAB) has been drilling on-shore on Öland and Gotland and off-shore east of Gotland. The only oil traps there have been reefs, which account for only three percent of world production. Both age and structure thus combine to make the Swedish side of the Baltic seabed an area of small promise, although minute quantities of oil have been found there.

New oil finds on the Soviet and Polish side of the Baltic seabed cannot be ruled out. The first test well was drilled in 1930 on the Polish coast. In 1975 the Soviet Union, Poland, and the German Democratic Republic formed a consortium, Petrobaltic, headquartered in Gdańsk to carry out joint hydrographic, geophysical, and seismic investigations in the southeastern part of the Baltic. An oil platform was built at a Dutch shipyard for Petrobaltic and started operations in 1980. On-shore production of oil has been reported since the late 1960s from small fields a Liepaya and Kaliningrad as well as from Gargzhdai in central Lithuania from a formation of Cambrian sandstone at a depth of 2,200 meters. In 1980 Poland had a blow out in an oil well near the Baltic coast. None of the fields, however, seems to produce more than a quarter of a million tons annually.

In the Danish-Polish Trough that runs from Poland, cuts across the southeastern corner of Skåne and central Sjaelland to Jutland, wildcat wells were drilled by the Swedish Geological Survey (SGU) in the early 1940s at Falsterbo, by the Danish American Prospecting Company (DAPCO) in the late 1950s in Sjaelland, and by OPAB in the early 1970s both on-shore and off-shore in Skåne. Over a dozen dry wells was the result. The Dansk Undergrunds Consortium (DUC), which until 1981 had the drilling rights on-shore and off-shore on Danish territory, found an interesting structure southwest of Bornholm, but no wells have yet been drilled.

The North German Basin, which barely reaches into the Baltic area, was investigated by DAPCO in the 1950's with half a dozen wildcats in southern Jutland and Lolland. DUC drilled in Falster. But no production resulted from all these prospecting activities. The Federal Republic of Germany has found some-oil off-shore near Kiel. The German Democratic Republic has a small producing field at Reinkenhagen south of Rügen in similar geological formations.

In sum, none of the oil-prospecting activities thus far indicates the Baltic will become a petroleum producing region of any significance.

With regard to mineral areas in the seabed, the chances of finding ores off-shore in the pre-Cambrian bedrock in the northern part of the Baltic area should be roughly the same as on-shore. Two such ore fields are known: First, the continuation of the Skellefte Field of sulfide ores, between Skellefteå and Oulu, and; second, the iron ores in the Åland Sea, which are extensions of the iron ores in Uppland, of worldwide reputation two hundred years ago but now produced in minor quantities. Along the Swedish east coast from Öland to Roslagen, north of Stockholm, there are indications of iron ore. Nodules containing iron and manganese but poor in copper and nickel are found on the seabed in the Baltic proper as well as in the Gulf of Bothnia and in the Gulf of Riga. Titanium and zirconium minerals, rutile and zircon, are present in heavy sands in Soviet waters at depths of three to eight meters, and an enterprise has been organized to mine them.

Sand and gravel are found in many places in the Baltic Sea and its approaches. A very large deposit covers the seabed around the northern part of Gotland, larger than anything found on-shore. Consumption of these construction materials is very large and growing in northwestern Europe. In Sweden it has grown by almost seven percent a year in recent decades. The on-shore excavation of eskers and other deposits in this sand-and-gravel-rich glaciated landscape has met increasing environmental opposition from a wide sector of the population who react to the ugly scars in the landscape, scars that become increasingly visible as more and more people drive between town and weekend homes. Some exploitation of seabed sand and gravel has taken place for many years, but a rapid switch from on-shore to off-shore exploitation seems very likely. Such exploitation should be preceded by basic research into environmental and legal consequences, especially for their effects upon the straits. Changes in the profile of the seabed may have important consequences for navigation as well as for the hydrology of the Baltic.

Amber is a very special mineral resource that historically has made the Baltic coast famous all over Europe and abroad. This fossil resin is still collected along the southern shores and used in jewelry, but it now ranks low among the products of the Baltic states. Two-thirds of the world's amber is produced in Kaliningrad Oblast and in Lithuania. Large collections are found in Kaliningrad and at Palanga north of Klaipeda as well as in the Hermitage of Leningrad and at the Armory of Moscow.[18]

Tourism and Recreation

The seacoast attracts people in search of recreation. Most coasts in densely populated Europe support a large tourist industry. Along the coasts of the sunny and warm Mediterranean and Black Sea large tourist hotels rim the sand beaches to which millions of people are brought by charter planes from colder and cloudier latitudes. But Europe has both a Sun Belt and a Frost

Belt. The Baltic seacoast undoubtedly is in the Frost Belt; nonetheless it plays an important part in the recreational life of the Frost Belt people.

In the summer, from June to August, the Baltic region has few counterparts elsewhere. The long days, the clear sky, the clean water, the fresh green, the pleasant climate, and the rocky or sandy coasts are most attractive to people in search of beauty and recreation. In no other country are second homes more common than in Denmark, Sweden, and Finland. Traditionally urban people in these three countries have lived in apartments, keeping a second home for summer use, preferably on or near the coast. The density of second homes is highest in the archipelagoes outside Stockholm, Turku, Helsinki, and on the coasts within easy reach of Copenhagen and Malmö. But metropolitan people may have second homes much farther away: for example, they are the largest group of second-home owners in the large islands of Åland, Gotland, Öland, and Bornholm where recreation and tourism are by far the most important sources of income. With increasing mobility, better roads, faster cars, and weekend buses, urban residents are increasingly using their second homes as weekend homes. In some cases, professional people have switched and made the house in the country their home and the apartment in the city their overnight place.

The high priority given to recreation was a major factor behind the radical switch from construction of apartments to the building of one-family homes in Sweden in the 1970s. Small towns of fewer than 10,000 inhabitants were preferred and especially those along the coast.[19] Unprecedented inflation and excessively high marginal taxes helped bring about the explosive growth in pleasure boat ownership. As houses went up in price, mortgages could be more easily obtained for a bank loan to buy a boat with loan interest deducted on tax returns. The per capita ownership of sailboats and other pleasure boats in Sweden probably exceeds any other country.

The short summer season makes it difficult to operate hotels and motels profitably in the tourist areas. Caravans, pleasure boats, tents and overnight cottages are used by temporary visitors in addition to the limited hotel and motel capacity. Families from abroad often rent a house on a weekly basis through their travel agency. A special form of recreation is offered by the ferries on some routes in the Baltic. The daily tours by large ferries, such as these between Stockholm and Mariehamn, Åland (10,000 inhabitants), are not required by the number of travellers between the two cities, except in midsummer. By far most passengers in the winter are retired people from Stockholm who take the day-trip to eat, drink, dance, play cards, meet friends and enjoy themselves, paying a very low ticket price and buying custom-free tobacco and liquor.

Chapter 3

THE BALTIC STATES

The Baltic region over the last millenium has seen frequent shifts in national boundaries. Many cities and counties have changed their allegiance, often several times. Two core areas, however, have remained independent units for a millenium: central Denmark and central Sweden. Norway over many centuries was a part of Denmark and Finland was a part of Sweden. The dynastic union under the Danish Queen Margrethe, known as the Kalmar Union (1389-1523), encompassed roughly the territories of all the present Nordic countries, including Greenland and Iceland. This region has been locally known as Norden (Scandinavia, Finland, Iceland, and Greenland), but the legality of the union was contested by Swedish nationalists, renewing a series of Danish-Swedish wars in the following three hundred years.

Denmark, the North-German cities (the Hanseatic League), the Teutonic Order and Sweden played prominent roles in the southeastern quadrant of the Baltic region for hundreds of years, at times cooperating with Poland and Lithuania in holding back Russian penetration of the Baltic area. The collapse of Sweden's Baltic empire and the emergence of Russia under Tsar Peter as a Great Power in Europe as a result of the Great Nordic War (1700-1721) finally created a new political situation in the Baltic region.

Population data had been kept as state secrets, but there could have been no doubts in the inquiring minds of Europe that the Danish and Swedish kings, although ruling over vast territories and laying claim to enormous bodies of water, had few inhabitants in their lands in comparison with several countries on the continent. Russia and Prussia in the eighteenth century emerged as great powers, not only in the Baltic region but in Europe and the world. Both based their claim to greatness on their armies rather than their navies; both were more prominent as producers (agriculture, mining, manufacturing) than traders and their merchant marines were rather small. It was not until the decades before the First World War that Germany, united in 1871, became a challenge to Britain as an industrial nation, a naval power, and a hub of world trade. Although Russia was immense in area and rich in potential natural resources, it was several decades behind western Europe in economic and social development.

For Germany and Russia in the early twentieth century, the Baltic region was just another area of conflict. Russia maintained an alliance with France, as both powers feared the strength of Germany, and the Russian defeat in Asia made possible its rapprochement with Britain. Germany meanwhile strengthened its fleet, made its influence felt in Asia as well as in Africa, and led the Triple Alliance with Austria-Hungary and Italy. The Scandinavian countries managed to remain neutral during World War I (1914-1918) as Germany and Russia fought their landwar south of the Baltic, but in World War II (1939-1945), Denmark was overrun and occupied by Germany; Norway resisted and was defeated by Germany; and only Sweden maintained a precarious neutrality between the Allied and Axis Forces.

Sweden

Through most of its history Sweden has been a major Baltic state. It has the longest coast line of all the littoral states of the Baltic Sea, and until the modern revolution in land transport - as long as land separated and water united - the Swedish capital was in a key, central position for the region. For most of its history Sweden was in conflict with Denmark, the other major Baltic state, sitting astride the entrance to Northern Europe's large, enclosed sea.

Most of the Swedish Vikings went eastward. On the island of Gotland alone, some 200,000 Arabic coins have been found. By way of the Volga River and the Caspian Sea the Vikings were in contact with the Caliphate of Baghdad, which reached the peak of its power during the Viking era. By way of the Dnepr River and the Black Sea the Vikings went to Byzantium.

The definite end of the Kalmar Union came with Gustav Vasa, who founded the Vasa Dynasty in 1523, turned Sweden into a Lutheran country, and marks the beginning of the modern period in Swedish history.

Swedish expansion south of the Gulf of Finland started with the conquest of Estonia in 1561 followed by Ingermanland and parts of Latvia in 1617. By the Treaty of Westphalia (1648), marking the end of the Thirty Years War in Germany, Sweden made large additional territorial gains on the southern coast of the Baltic as well as the North Sea coast, including Bremen. Sweden became one of the Great Powers of Europe. Two treaties with Denmark, at Brömsebro (1645) and Roskilde (1658), established the present boundaries with Denmark and Norway, a sizeable increase of the Swedish territory, including Skåne, Blekinge, Halland, Bohuslän, as well as the island of Gotland in the south and Jämtland further to the north. Sweden reached its maximum extension in 1658.

Sweden has faced two seas since the seventeenth century: the East Sea (Sw. *Östersjön*), or the Baltic, and the West Sea (Sw. *Västerhavet*), a term sometimes used for the Kattegat and the Skagerrak.[1] Eventually, with the relative decline of the Baltic in world affairs, this had a profound impact on the population distribution of the country. With the advent of the Industrial Revolution and the construction of railroads after 1850, the trunk line system built by the Swedish government had a pronounced West Coast bias. But the seventeenth century governments had a strong Baltic interest, and the new naval base (Karlskrona), built after 1680, was located in the southeastern corner of the country.

Most of the territory south of the Gulf of Finland was lost during the Great Nordic War. By the Treaty of Fredrikshamn (1809), Sweden had to cede Finland to Russia, and by the Treaty of Kiel (1814) the last small German territories were lost. By the Kiel Treaty, moreover, the Swedish Crown Prince Karl-Johan (Bernadotte), Napoleon's former Marshal, succeeded in breaking up the old union between Denmark and Norway and instead arranging a dynastic union between Sweden and Norway.

The Treaty of Kiel marked the beginning of an unbroken peace period for Sweden up to the present. But it did not mark the beginning of Swedish neutrality. King Oscar I was weary of Russian expansionism and under certain conditions would have given up Sweden's neutrality to join Britain and France in the Crimean War. But he thought the Western powers were attacking 'the little toe of the Giant' (Crimea) instead of 'the throat' (St. Petersburg). The King also feared that the Russians wanted to take the Varangerfjord from Norway to get access to icefree harbors. Since this would threaten Britain, in 1855 Lord Palmerston offered Western guarantees for the integrity of the Norwegian Arctic coast. In the 1855 November Treaty Sweden and Norway promised not to give up any territory or grant any grazing or fishing rights to Russia. If the Scandinavians were faced with such demands the Western powers promised to provide Sweden-Norway with military aid.[2]

The loss of Finland in 1809 made Sweden an exceptionally homogeneous nation in language, religion and political identity. Social and economic problems became the core of political debate, not border disputes or the position of religious and linguistic minorities as in many other countries of Europe. The awakening of Finnish nationalism was followed at a distance. It no longer was a problem for Stockholm but for St. Petersburg. Feelings in Sweden were pro-Finland but not necessarily pro-Finnish. Nationalist authors in Finland, primarily Runeberg and Topelius, were as much read and appreciated in Sweden as in their home country. Swedish opninion became strongly anti-Russian when the Russification program in Finland got under way in the 1890s. The Swedish-speaking population in Finland retained close ties with the old mother country but in times of crisis always remained loyal to Helsinki.

The awakening of nationalism in Norway, which had been part of Denmark since 1380, preceded the personal union with Sweden. The Norwegians adopted a constitution at Eidsvoll on 17 May, 1814 (now Norway's National

Day) and proclaimed an independent Norway. Out of the events of 1814 came the personal union under the Swedish king with almost complete autonomy for Norway. Oslo or, as it was then known, Kristiania, succeeded distant Bergen as the capital. As a concession to the union, the flags of each country carried the flag of the other country in a corner while consular representation abroad was common. Even these small limitations eventually were felt as restraints by the Norwegians, especially after the conspicuous expansion of the Norwegian fleet of sailing vessels during and after the American Civil War. Norway became an exporter of transport services to the world market and wanted to sail under the "pure flag" and have its own Norwegian consuls in world ports. This conflict led to the peaceful dissolution of the union in 1905.

As indicated before, Sweden has the longest Baltic coast line among the seven littoral states. However, the west-orientation of Sweden's foreign trade makes the short west coast, facing the Kattegat and the Skagerrak, especially Gothenburg, stand out as the leading district of port oriented industry and port activity, particularly if the Swedish side of the Sound is included. The two major ports here, Helsingborg and Malmö, compete with Stockholm for second place among Swedish general cargo ports, ferry traffic not included.

In Gothenburg the Baltic coast is often referred to as the "backside" of the country, a joking reference to the considerable relative decline over the latest 150 years of southeastern Sweden. The Russian October Revolution of 1917 and the creation of a new economic system in Eastern Europe that temporarily made the Soviet Union more inwardlooking than the old Tsarist Empire did little to slow up the tilting of the Swedish economy away from the Baltic. This tendency continued after World War II when Balticum − the collective name for Estonia, Latvia, and Lithuania − and the land south of the Baltic, all the way to the gates of Lübeck, came under Soviet economic domination.[3]

A recent increase in East-West trade has undoubtedly benefited the ports on the Swedish east coast more than those on the west coast. However, Sweden's transit position for trade with the Soviet Union and Poland should not be exaggerated, for traffic handled in Swedish ports has finally been generated in the Scandinavian Peninsula. The state railroad trunk line system, built after the middle of last century, gave a strong bias to west coast development but the lessening of the role of railroads in the Swedish transportation system is favoring the population along the southeastern coast. Road traffic has continued to expand at the expense of rail traffic, so that population curves for coastal areas in the southeast are again positive after decades of decline.[4]

However, the west coast of Sweden has traditionally been much more important than the east coast for the fishing industry, but in recent years many west coast trawlers have operated out of Baltic ports. The new economic zones have squeezed out Swedish fishermen on the west coast but are generous to Sweden on the east coast.

Finland

The Finnish way to a national identity among the states of Europe was long and tortuous. For some six hundred years before 1809 Finland was an integrated province of Sweden and then became an autonomous Grand Duchy under the Russian Tsar. During Finland's first twenty-one years of independence, from 1918 to 1939, the country experienced social conflict internally and insecurity in foreign relations, but it also made remarkable progress in the development of some export industries. The traumatic experiences of Finland during the Second World War seem to have given the small state a cohesion and stability that in the post-World-War II period have gained it respect in the international community, but not the least among her neighbors.

Although farthest of all the coastal states from the Baltic Straits, Finland deserves study as a unique bridge state between East and West in the greater balance of power system of the world. Its economic system, international relations, and its culture make it a western nation; its geography and history make it a bridge state.

In bilingual Finland the Swedish-speaking minority long was dominant in political and economic affairs. The Swedes probably reached their largest share of the country's population in the fourteenth century; in 1749 they made up 22 percent; and in 1880 people reporting Swedish as their mother tongue still made up 14 percent of the population: 38 percent in the small urban sector and 12 percent in the rural areas. Because of their lower birth rates and higher emigration rates, as well as their intermarriage with the Finnish-speaking majority, the Swedes in Finland gradually were reduced to seven percent of the population in 1970.[5]

Prehistoric Finland was inhabited by Laps. The Nordic name of the country, Finland, literally means the land of the Laps. The Finns belong to the Finno-Ugrian group of people who moved from their place of origin, straddling the lower Volga River, to their present home area in the first millenium after Christ. Migrating over the Gulf of Finland, these people were hunters, fishermen, and farmers with a culture well adapted to the forest and lake landscape of interior Finland. The Swedes followed their old trade route to the east through the archipelago along the north coast of the Gulf of Finland, settling and trading with the Finns in the interior.

Åbo (Turku), facing Stockholm, became the leading city of Finland. A university, Åbo Academy, was established here in 1640. Finnish nationalism was rooted at Åbo Academy where H.G. Porthan (1739-1804) and other teachers, often of Swedish-speaking background, devoted their research to unravel the history, language and culture of the Finns. At the time of the French Revolution (1789), the small educated class in Finland was nationally conscious.

This eastern province of the Swedish realm was often ravaged in the wars with Russia, especially in the Great Nordic War (1700-1721) when the whole province was occupied by the Russians.

During the Napoleonic Wars, Alexander I of Russia made a deal with the French Emperor at Tilsit in 1807, accepting the spheres of influence suggested by Napoleon. Alexander promised to participate in the blockade of Britain in exchange for a free hand against Sweden.

Prompted by Napoleon, Alexander in 1808 attacked Finland, encountering little resistance, and declared that he would make Finland a Russian province. Because Swedish military policy was in the hands of the inept Gustav IV Adolf, the Finns were left to fend for themselves. Soldiers and subaltern officers loyal to the Swedish Crown started to fight back; in occupied areas guerila-warfare broke out. Faced with a situation in Europe in which Napoleon might soon be again ready for an attack, Alexander I wanted to extricate his forces from the war in Finland and settled for making the area a Grand Duchy, ruled independently of the Empire.

As a Russian Grand Duchy, Finland enjoyed fairly unrestricted autonomy during most of the nineteenth century. The university was moved from Åbo to Helsingfors (Helsinki) in 1828, after a great fire, and Helsinki became the capital. The association with Russia offered advantages for some sectors of the Finnish economy, not the least for the small Finnish industry. Foreign, primarily British, and domestic interests in the textile industry got started at the waterfalls of Tampere at an earlier stage and on a larger scale than elsewhere in the Nordic countries. The Finnish merchant marine was not large in a Nordic context but is was larger than the Russian merchant fleet during most of the nineteenth century. Last but not least: Finland under Russian rule enjoyed a hundred years of peace, the only exception being the presence of the British navy in Finnish waters during the Crimean War, and the constitution of 1772 established by Gustaf III of Sweden served Finland relatively well in her association with the autocratic empire.

From about 1860 the nationalistic movement in Finland intensified, and in 1863 the Finnish language advocates succeeded in having a manifesto signed by the Russian Grand Duke to make Finnish within twenty years an official language with Swedish in all matters relating to the Finnish-speaking majority, ending the need for a Finn to learn Swedish in order to join the small educated group.[6]

Finland in the nineteenth century lived quite independently of the mainstream of the contemporary Russian society. However, in the 1890s the Russian tsars showed that they would renege on the promises of their predecessors to respect the Finnish constitution and Finland's special position as associated with rather than part of the Russian Empire. The situation came to a crisis level with the appointment of Nicholas Bobrikov as Governor General in 1898 and the signing by Nicholas II of the February Manifesto in 1899, which extended the absolute power of the Tsar to Finland. Civil servants loyal to the laws of Finland were dismissed and in their positions came Russophiles and Russians. Freedom af speech, association and meeting were abolished. Russian was made Finland's official language and the main subject in schools. Finland's own military forces were disbanded.

A passive resistance movement, recruited among civil servants and teachers in key positions, was organized in the secret *Kagalen,* which later was to play an important role in Finland's fight for independence.[7] The uprisings in Russia, following the Russo-Japanese War 1904-1905, created hope in Finland, but a new crisis in the relations between Russia and Finland came in 1909 when the Russification program was further advanced.

During World War I the Russians kept troops in Finland, for the enemy was expected to attempt an occupation of the Grand Duchy, where the Russophobe feelings were quite strong. The February Revolution in Petrograd (March 1917) and the abdication of the Tsar led to a restored Finnish autonomy. But by then autonomy was not sufficient for political parties in Finland and they sought independence. The October Revolution (November 1917) brought V.I. Lenin to power in Petrograd. In his writings he had advocated the principle of national self-determination. On 8 December 1917, the *Lantdag* unanimously adopted the Finnish declaration of independence, which in January 1918 was accepted by the new Russian government. France, Germany, and the Scandinavian countries, followed by other governments, entered into diplomatic relations with the new country, but Britain and the United States waited till the following year.

After independence Finland faced a terribly confused situation, complicated by the continuing war between Germany and the western allies as well as the civil struggles in Russia between the Bolsheviks and the White Guard. From the end of January 1918 Finland was involved in a war of liberation, alternatively called a civil war or an uprising, which obviously had strong elements of both. The White, supporting the legal government, stood against the Reds, organized by a radical fraction of the Social Democrats, who later formed the Communist Party.

Both sides in the uprising were supported from outside, the Red Guards by Russia and the Rangers (Whites), who had been trained in Germany, became officers in the government forces. Although both sides were poorly armed and the uprising was of short duration, the deaths were a staggering 31,500, or about one percent of the population, of which one-third died in the prison camps and almost one-third were executed.

The government in October 1918 invited Prince Frederic Charles of Hessen to become King of Finland, but after Germany's collapse, the Prince declined the offered throne and the German-oriented government in Finland was followed by one led by General C.G.E. Mannerheim, who had good relations with the western powers. In the constitution, adopted in 1919, Finland was made an independent republic and the first president was elected the same year. The Treaty of Dorpat (1920) was similar to the peace treaties signed by Russia with the Baltic republics about the same time.

During the 1920s there were strong anti-Communist feelings in Finland, which in 1929 found their expression in the Lappo Movement that got wide support, but soon was controlled by extremists. Terrorism was directed against Communist printing shops and individuals. Prominent politicians from other parties, including and former president and his wife, were forcefully "transported" to the Russian border and left there to find their way home. The Lappo Movement ended with an armed uprising 1932. However, it was dissolved before the shooting had started. The relations between Finland and the Soviet Union remained cool because of mutual suspicions. The Finns feared the loss of their independence and the Soviet Union was aware that Finland's territory in a war could be used as a base of operation against the Russian heartland since Leningrad was only 32 km from the Finnish border. Relations with the Soviet Union were strained also in the economic field. Estonia had five times and Sweden seven times Finland's share in the foreign trade of the Soviet Union in the interwar years.

At the end of World War I, Sweden expected war operations in the Baltic. To protect the security of the capital, Swedish troops occupied the Åland Islands, seventy-five miles from Stockholm. When the Swedes had withdrawn, Germany sent troops to the islands to secure the logistics of German forces in Finland, which were there on the request of the Finnish government. Relations between Finland and Sweden were also strained during the 1920's, for they each claimed the Åland Islands. In 1922 the League of Nations decided that the islands had no right to a plebiscite on their independence, contrary to Sweden's claim, but that they should be neutralized, unfortified, and not used by Finland as a military base. Sweden's refusal, moreover, during World War I to train Finnish soldiers, the outspoken sympathy shown by the Social Democrats for the Reds as well as its favor of the Finnish Social Democrats during the legal proceedings following the civil war embittered many Finns. The language conflict was another source of irritation between the two countries.

In the 1930's Finland became interested in cooperation with small nations in Europe, and especially the other Nordic countries, which had remained neutral during the First World War. The seven "Oslo states", which in addition to the four Nordic countries included the Netherlands, Belgium, and Luxemburg, declared their intention to stay neutral in a future European conflict, but efforts to coordinate their defense failed.

Sweden and Finland in January 1939 had finally signed an agreement about fortifications in the Åland Islands, which was submitted to the League of Nations for approval, but the Soviet Union objected on the grounds that such fortifications could be used in an attack on Leningrad. The League of Nations never came to a decision on the issue, and all discussion ended with the beginning of World War II on 1 September 1939.

The Soviet Union in the early fall of 1939, after the collapse of Poland, called the ministers of foreign affairs in Estonia, Latvia, and Lithuania to Moscow for negotiations about Soviet military bases in each country. Under threat, these demands were met. Later the Finnish government was similarly invited to send a negotiator to Moscow. However, the Finns did not yield any territory, and on 30 November, Soviet troops went over the border in the Karelian Isthmus. In the Soviet version, the Finnish troops had started the shooting, but that story was not believed outside Russia. The Russo-German negotiations and the diplomatic activity in the late prewar and early war years can be followed through the German state papers published soon after the German collapse in 1945 by the victors.[8]

Some commentators have questioned the wisdom of the Finnish government in not accomodating reasonable Soviet demands for strategic bases for the defense of Leningrad. However, this should be considered in the contemporary European setting. Poland had just been partitioned between Germany and the Soviet Union and the Baltic Republics had had their defense positions severely weakened by admitting foreign military personnel onto their territory. In a few months they were to be invaded by Soviet troops. Finland was another pawn in the jockeying for positions by the two Great Powers which in spite of the Ribbentrop Pact of August 1939 were mutually suspicious of each other.[9]

Germany observed strict neutrality in the Soviet-Finnish war but Sweden never declared its neutrality in the Winter War of 1939-1940. It was "nonbelligerent" and supported Finland with weapons and war material. Finnish children and crippled soldiers were evacuated to Sweden and a corps of volunteers was recruited and sent to the front at the end of the war. In the early days of the Winter War, Sweden got a broadly based coalition government. The secretary of foreign affairs, Rickard Sandler, had wanted to implement the Stockholm Plan and help Finland build fortifications in the Åland Islands but did not get support for his view in the government and resigned.[10] The Swedish government in February turned down a Finnish request for voluntary army units. Finland then pinned its hope on France and Britain, which decided to send troops to Finland by way of Narvik and Lapland, but the governments of Norway and Sweden refused the transit of British and French troops, which forced Finland to accept the harsh conditions of the Treaty of Moscow (12 March 1940).

The Treaty of Moscow did not stabilize the relations between the two countries. The war was continued in the diplomatic and political field. During this war of nerves the Finns were under the impression that their big neighbor just waited for the right moment to crush the independence of Finland, as demonstrated by the occupation of the Baltic republics in the summer of 1940. The German occupation of Denmark and Norway in April, 1940, moreover, strengthened Finnish isolation and made its renewed neutrality policy less credible.

In August 1940, Finland agreed to let the Soviet Union send military personnel on Finnish railroads between the Hanko military base - on territory leased by the Russians - and the Soviet border. The agreement contained detailed rules about the number of soldiers, amount of weapons, type of transports, and so forth. About the same time Sweden yielded to German requests for similar transit between the Norwegian border and ports on the Swedish south coast. They were also strictly regulated and claimed to be consistent with the Swedish policy of neutrality. Somewhat later Finland agreed to allow German soldiers on home-leave to travel through northern Finland on their way to and from Norway, but no limits were set on the number of soldiers that were allowed to be in Finland simultaneously. Thus, the two Great Powers preparing for a war on an eastern front both shipped troops through Finland. To uphold a credible neutrality under those circumstances would have required Finnish armed forces far beyond the carrying capacity of the country. In the spring of 1941 Finnish public opinion showed sympathy for Germany and animosity tainted by fear for the Soviet Union.

After the German attack on 22 June 1941 German bombers from airfields south of the Baltic followed the southern coast of Finland on their way to Leningrad. The Red Army, under the assumption that the planes came from Finland, started operations on the Finnish front. Although military preparations in Finland and the positioning of troops were aimed for an attack, the civilian authorities were undecided, yet, faced with a fait accompli, the prime minister told the *Riksdag* that Finland now was at war with the Soviet Union, the War of Compensation (for the losses in the Winter War).

In the armistice agreement with the Soviet Union in September 1944, Finland accepted the peace treaty of 1940 and agreed to withdraw its troops behind the frontiers then agreed upon. Airfields in southern Finland were made available to the Soviet airforce for operations against the Germans in Estonia and in the northern part of the Baltic; the Porkala Peninsula southwest of Helsinki (380 km²) was leased to the Soviet Union for 50 years; Finland was to pay war reparations at a value of US $300 million within six years; and payments were to be in the form of deliveries from the Finnish manufacturing industry. A final peace treaty was signed in Paris in February 1947, which confirmed the demilitarization of the Åland Islands and established a maximum size for Finland's armed forces.

The transition from war to peace turned out to be difficult. Mannerheim as President, J.K. Paasikivi as Prime Minister, and C. Enckell as Foreign Secretary had to solve difficult Finnish political and economic problems in cooperation with the Soviet Union. They developed what has later been known as the Paasikivi line for East-West peaceful cooperation, a line that was later continued by U.K. Kekkonen, who was several times elected as Finland's President.

The war reparations were a heavy burden on the Finnish economy. They had been fixed at US $300 million in the 1938 world market prices. Although the Soviet Union accepted a reduction with $73.5 million, the value in 1952 prices was some $550 million. To pay the reparations Finland had to expand its engineering industry, especially its shipyards (icebreakers, passenger vessels) and plants producing machinery and other equipment for the forest industries. To maintain employment in these plants after reparations had been paid, Finland entered into long-term bilateral trade agreements with its eastern neighbor for a commodity exchange at world market prices. In the beginning Finland had a positive trade which only with great efforts could be balanced. In spite of its small size, Finland was long the leading trade partner in the West of the Soviet Union. The mutual confidence that gradually developed between the two countries in 1955 led the Russians to return the Porkala area to Finland.[11] At the same time the friendship and mutual assistance pact of 1948 was renewed for twenty years.

Finland's admission to the United Nations was not granted until 1955 when Krushchev established the policy of peaceful coexistence for the Soviet Union. "Finlandization" has become a term often used by westerners to indicate that the Soviet Union is exerting pressure on nominally independent states. The Finns have resented this usage, insisting that they have learned to live in the shadow of Russia without giving up their political and economic system, and noting that the West has never been in a position to guarantee Finland's security. Finland's geopolitical situation is unique and so is the Finnish security policy.[12]

Finland has a long coast line on the Baltic Sea, surpassed only by Sweden and the Soviet Union. Like Poland and East Germany, Finland has only one coast, but in contrast to these countries the coastal fringe is economically the most advanced part of the nation. The economic core area, marked by the big city triangle Helsinki-Turku-Tampere in the southeast, is a centerpiece of the dominating coastal rim. Like Sweden, Norway, and the Danish islands, Finland is a trans-Baltic country seen from the West-European core region. Surface connections for passengers and general cargo are by way of Sweden or directly by ferry to the Lübeck area. The Helsinki-Travemünde route is served by the world's largest passenger ferry.

No country holds a larger share of the world population living north of latitude 60°N than Finland, about 35 percent. Only a tiny corner of the country, in the southwest, extends south of this latitude. The Gulf of Finland and the Gulf of Bothnia in contrast to the Baltic Sea proper are regularly covered by ice in the winter, which means that Finland until the end of last century was isolated from the rest of western Europe for a long period every year. Since the 1890's, icebreakers have made it possible to keep sea lanes open to two ports in the southeast, Hanko and Turku. Export products from the forest industry districts along the coast in the east and north were carried by rail to these two ports, making winter a busy period for the Finnish railroads. In recent decades, Finland has become a builder of icebreakers to the world market and the large icebreakers of today make it possible to keep more ports open to shipping throughout the winter.

In the manufacturing sector Finland no longer is dominated by its forest industries, for the production value of the engineering industry equals that of the old base of the Finnish economy. Finland has a much higher percentage of its gainfully employed population on farms than Denmark, and politically the small farmers' party has always been important in Finland. The demographic transition to low birth and death rates has gone further in Finland than in the other Nordic countries. Finland used to have the highest birth rates, now it vies with Sweden about the lowest. In all countries and Soviet republics bordering the Baltic, the birthrates are generally below reproduction rates.

As in Norway and Sweden, the northern regions of Finland are economic problem areas. An "active location" policy has been carried out in recent years in all three countries. Saw mills, pulp and paper plants, and mines at the end of the nineteenth century had lured people from the south to the mushrooming towns of the North along the coasts of Sweden and Finland, for new jobs. The export-oriented forest industry along the coast gave temporary employment to an even larger number of inland people cutting and hauling the logs in the winter and floating them down the rivers in the spring and early summer. The rest of the year the lumbermen helped their families on their small farms. This system was satisfactory until the late 1950's in Sweden and somewhat longer in Finland. To meet the demand for a higher standard of living (higher real wages) the large forest companies then had to mechanize cutting and transportation which meant a tremendous reduction in the number of jobs. A group of machine-operators took over on a full-time basis. Lumber no longer was floated but hauled by truck or train to the coastal factories.

The unemployed lumbermen were retrained for jobs primarily in the engineering and construction industries in Stockholm and other cities of central Sweden and Southern Finland. Many moved to cities along the coast in the

Table 4

Population and Land Area of States in the Baltic Region

State	Population 1979 Millions	Land area Thousands of km^2	Population per km^2
Sweden	8.3	450.0	18
Finland	4.8	337.0	14
Soviet Union	262.4	22402.0	12
In Europe	183.1*	5571.0	33
RSFSR	137.6	17074.0	8
Estonian SSR	1.5	45.1	33
Latvian SSR	2.5	63.7	39
Lithuanian SSR	3.4	65.2	52
Kaliningrad Oblast	0.8	15.1	53
Poland	35.4	312.7	113
GDR (East Germany)**	16.7	108.2	154
FRG (West Germany)**	61.3	248.6	247
Denmark	5.1	43.1	118

Sources: United Nations, Monthly Bulletin of Statistics, July 1977.
United Nations, Statistical Yearbook 1975.
Narodnoe Chosjaistvo SSSR v. 1975 g.
Geojournal Supplementary Issue 1(1980), Soviet Census 1979

* 1970

** Include relevant data for Berlin "without prejudice to any question of status which may be involved" (UN).

north. There was also a large migration from the forest districts of northern Finland to central Sweden. Within the common Nordic labor market (1954) Finnish citizens had no difficulties except psychological ones (stemming from unsatisfactory knowledge of Swedish) in obtaining jobs in the more rewarding Swedish labor market. In Sweden, an area roughly north of a line from Gävle over Filipstad to Arvika was classified as "support area" eligible for government help in obtaining new job-creating industry. An interior zone was singled out as in special need of help. The population development in the interior zone was unfavorable in the 1960's and early 70s while the coastal fringe was able to hold its own. In Finland these structural changes came later and were less dramatic but nonetheless evident.

The problem of the north obviously is most striking in the extreme north: the periphery of the periphery in the three peripheral countries. The "top" of Europe, roughly an area north of an east-west line through the innermost part of the Gulf of Bothnia, is known as the North Calotte. It has a very low population density but the traditional density measure (inh/km^2) has little meaning today in highly industrialized countries where four-fifths of the population live in urban places, small islands in a virtually empty sea. In the North Calotte, places are very small and far between. The largest place in the Nordic portion of the Calotte is the trading center Rovaniemi (29,000 inh) in the Finnish Lapland, somewhat larger than the Swedish mining towns Kiruna (25,000) and Gällivare (18,000). Places of one or two thousand inhabitants are important regional centers in this part of Europe.

The geographic position of Norway, Sweden, and Finland in relation to the West European core, however, is more favorable than appears from a map, since population and industrial capacity in all three countries is strongly concentrated in the south.

Soviet Union

The centrally planned economy established in Russia after November 1917 was the first national attempt to test the principles of Karl Marx and V.I. Lenin. The Baltic border regions in the west, from Finland to Poland took advantage of the positive writings of Lenin about national self-determination and of the military weakness of post-revolutionary Russia and declared their independence. The USSR was left with only "a window to the West".[13] The Finnish border was barely 32 km from Petrograd and the Estonian border some 140 km.

Russia had become an empire and great power in Europe under Peter the Great, whose victory over Charles XII in the Great Nordic War (1700-1721) brought an end to Sweden's preeminence in the Baltic region. In 1712 St. Petersburg was made the capital of Russia, for Peter the Great placed great importance on contact with northwestern Europe and the modernization of the vast Russian Empire. This historic move occured only three years after the decisive Russian victory over the Swedish army at Poltava in the Ukraine and two years before the battle at Hangö, the first naval victory in Russian history. The transfer of the capital was also intended to get away from the strong old-Russian influence in Moscow.

The treaty of Nystad 1721 provided Russia with a secure frontage on the Baltic from Viborg to Riga: Karelia, Ingria, Estonia, and Livonia were ceded by Sweden. Through St. Petersburg the Western technology flooded into Russia. Before, it had but seeped through joints and cracks. The largest crack traditionally had been Livonia with Riga as the great emporium. St. Petersburg became not only the center of government but the financial and commercial capital as well. Arkhangel lost its privileges and was reduced to insignificance.

Peter's new galley fleet, built while Charles XII neglected his eastern provinces for other strategies, by 1725 consisted of some 800 vessels manned by 28,000 sailors. Contrary to expectations, Russia did not become a major naval power, for after Peter's death the number of seaworthy naval vessels in the Baltic dwindled to insignificance. The Russian merchant marine also remained unimportant until the end of the empire in 1917.

The name of Peter's capital was russified to Petrograd after the outbreak of hostilities with Germany in 1914. After the death of Lenin in 1924, the city was again renamed, now to Leningrad.

Before the Mongol invasion of the thirteenth century, Kiev had been the cradle of the Russian nationality. Like Novgorod further to the north it was on the Viking communication line between the Baltic and the Byzantine capital (Constantinople) by way of the Neva, the Volkhov, and the Dnepr. In the ninth century the Swedish Vikings or Varangians, many of whom were from the Roslagen district north of Stockholm, had a colony south of Ladoga with centers at Staraja and at Novgorod. The early Russian as well as Greek and Arab know them as the Rus, Rhos, or Rusi, from which is derived the name of the country, Russia.[14] The social organization and the legal system of medieval Kiev and Novgorod show similarities with the contemporary systems in Denmark and Sweden.[15]

Unlike Kiev, Novgorod was never occupied by the Mongols. For centuries it was a cosmopolitan Grand Duchy, a kind of city republic, governed by boyars and merchants, among whom those of the Hanseatic League were prominent. Its influence stretched to the Artic Ocean in the north and far to the east. In the west, Novgorod claimed parts of Estonia, Livonia, and Finland, which led to wars with the Teutonic Order and Sweden. In 1240, Prince Alexander of Novgorod at the mouth of the Neva crushed a Swedish fleet, attempting to block Novgorod's access to the sea, and became known in Russian history as Alexander Nevsky.

Arkhangel on the White Sea had been Russia's first access to the sea. It was used by the Muscovite Trading Company of London, established at the end of the sixteenth century during the reign of Elizabeth I. The Principality of Moscow at that time became the core of the Great Russian nation, which emerged during the upheavels that followed the medieval Mongol or Tatar invasion. Arkhangel long was the only seaport under Russian control. Sweden had a firm hold on both shores of the Gulf of Finland after 1561 when the German knights dissolved the Order that for over 300 years had held a large section of the Baltic littoral. Ivan the Dread, the first Russian Tsar, had invaded the Order's territory and Estonia asked for Swedish protection. The head of the Gulf came under Swedish control in 1617 when Ingria, or Inger-manland, was conquered.

The second sea outlet of modern Russia was established on the Pacific coast when Great Russian fur hunters, merchants, and explorers pushing eastward through almost empty Siberia, reached the remote shore after 1639. For a long time, ports in the far eastern part of the Empire were of little importance for the Russian economy.

In the southeast, astride the middle Dnepr, the little Russian nation or Ukraine had developed by the 16th century. It had Kiev as its capital. In the basin of the upper Dnepr was the White Russian nation (Minsk). Both had their own form of Slavic tongue. They were under the political control of Lithuania - Poland, that once stretched from the Baltic to the Black Sea. Po-land and Turkey, which in 1683 in the decisive battle at Vienna was prevented by the Polish King Jan Sobieski from overrunning western Europe, had preempted the land north of the Black Sea. For three centuries before the re-gime of Peter the Great, Russia thus was detached from Europe and displaced into Asia.

It was not until 1772 that Russia came into possession of Odessa and the Crimea and thus became a Black Sea power. In the Treaty of Kutchuk-Kainardji (1774), Turkey was forced by Catherine II of Russia to open up the Black Sea and the Strait of the Dardanelles to Russian merchant vessels. After the Turkish conquest of Constantinople in 1453, the Black Sea had been a Turkish inland sea. According to the "ancient rule of the Ottoman Empire", foreign warships were not admitted into the Strait as long as the Porte was at peace. Merchant vessels were excluded in the distrection of the Porte.[16] For nearly 500 years the Russians intermittently fought the Turks. In the nine-teenth century the fate of the Ottoman Empire, including the use of the Strait of Dardanelles dominated Russian and European politics.[17]

The icefree port of Murmansk (69°N) on the North Calotte was a late addi-tion to the series of Russian gateways to the sea. It was established during World War I to secure supplies from the Western allies. The all year ports on the coast of the Barents Sea are kept open by the North Atlantic Drift, a branch of the Gulf Stream. These ports, and those in the White Sea, are on waters that cannot easily be closed off by an enemy.

Murmansk is the largest Soviet naval base (home of the North Fleet) and a ma-jor fishing port of a superpower with global ambitions. In addition, it is an im-portant mining area. Along with the Vladivostok-Nakhodka port complex in the Far East, Murmansk is the only Soviet port with exits to the world ocean that do not pass through narrow straits or canals. The city has more than 360,000 in-habitants with no peer in such high latitudes. High wages, twice the national average, compensate for two and a half months of polar night and ten months of snowfall. The existence of Murmansk makes the remote North Calotte a strate-gic key area in the world.

The Communist regime of Russia in the first chaotic years had a weak hold on the country. It was concentrating on its domestic problems, which were formidable after the long and devastating world war, the revolution, the civil war and the foreign intervention. Instead of "World revolution", preached by the Bolsheviks before the October events of 1917, came "socialism in one country" which was different from "National socialism".[18] A tier of nations along the western border of Russia (Poland, Lithuania, Latvia, Estonia, and Finland) declared their independence and, after a period of fighting and chaos, signed treaties with the new Russian government, regulating their independent status. Others were brought back into the fold.[19] The new border states were wary of the intentions of the Soviet Union when it had emerged out of the post-war disorder. Their political relations with the Soviet Union were strained throughout the interwar period for this reason. By Western Europe, these countries were seen as a buffer zone, a "cordon sanitaire", against the new Russia, the home of Comintern, which was considered subversive in the rest of the world.

Between World War I and World War II the Soviet Union did not do much to renew old trade ties with neighboring countries in the West. The capital of the Soviet Union in 1918 was moved from Petrograd to Moscow, one of many signs of a *de facto* isolationistic policy in the new union of socialist republics that succeeded the old empire after a short interlude of a parliamentary regime between the fall of the Tsarist Government in March and the Bolshevik October Revolution in November 1917.[20]

Governments and public opinion in the West viewed the new Russia with mixed feelings, for a "dictatorship of the proletariat" and "central economic planning" were unacceptable concepts in countries with a multiparty democracy and a market economy. In all western countries, political refugees, who had survived the Revolution and the Civil War in Russia, did little to reconcile citizens of the West with the new political and economic system of the Soviet Union. The United States did not recognize the Soviet government until 1933, by which time the German dictatorship of Adolf Hitler began to threaten western Europe.[21]

Russo-German weakness and a common disdain of the victors of World War I led to the Rapallo Agreement of 1922 that ruled the commercial relations between the two Baltic powers until 1933. Hitler's growing menace, however, gradually led to confrontation, and the Soviet Union became a member of the League of Nations, declaring that it accepted the Treaty of Versailles.

The Soviet territorial expansion in the Baltic region during the Second World War was striking. German command and influence was pressed back to the Oder River. At the expense of Finland, moreover, the Soviet Union advanced its boundaries in three sectors, of which the most important was in the Karelian Isthmus or the neck of land between the Gulf of Finland and Lake Ladoga. Among the ceded cities was Viborg (Viipuri), the old eastern outpost of the Swedish realm which had been ceded to Russia in the Treaty of Nystad in 1721 but again incorporated into Finland in 1812. In the interwar period, Viborg was one of Finland's two or three most important harbors due to its location at the sea-entrance of the Saima Canal.

The other two areas ceded by Finland were outside the Baltic region proper. One straddled the Arctic Circle in a sparsely populated wilderness region. The other was the nation's only outlet to ice-free water, the Petsamo corridor facing the Barents Sea. This region contained Europe's leading nickel mine, developed after 1934 by Mond Nickel Co., a subsidiary of Inco of Canada.

The Soviet Union, the largest country in the world, borders several seas from the Pacific in the east to the Baltic in the west. For the Soviet Union, the Baltic coast is a port district, second only to the Black Sea. The Baltic Fleet is third after the Northern and Pacific Fleets but the Baltic naval construction and repair yards rank first in the country. Petrograd and the Kronstadt naval base on an island in the Baltic played an important part in the October Revolution.

The Leningrad area has remained a leading repair and maintenance base for the Soviet navy. Leningrad is the headquarters of the Warsaw Pact naval command.

The importance of the Baltic as a shipbuilding area for the Soviet navy with its global ambitions was underlined in the late summer of 1980 when Swedish reconnaissance planes photographed two large warships on their test trips. One, the nuclear-powered battleship *Kirov*, built in Leningrad, with a displacement of 32,000 tons and a speed of some 30 knots, was said to be the most powerful marine unit for its tonnage built in the world. The ship carried launch pads for strategic nuclear missiles, the latest anti-submarine missiles, and three types of guidance radar.

The second ship sailing along with the *Kirov* was previously unknown in the West. It was a heavy destroyer, with a displacement of some 5,000 tons, carrying helicopters for submarine chase and equipped with sophisticated gear for the guidance of missiles and guns for targets on the sea and the sky.

Leningrad is the second largest city in the Soviet Union and by far the largest metropolis on the Baltic. As a general cargo port it is somewhat larger than Odessa in the south. The port became one of the two major outlets for the vast Russian coniferous forest belt, competing with Arkhangel and some smaller timber ports on the White Sea. Leningrad is connected by an interior waterway system with the White Sea, the Caspian Sea and the Black Sea. "Volgo-Balt" river boats (3,000 grt) in recent years have hauled logs to sawmills in southern Sweden and other cargo from the interior of Russia to ports on the North Sea and vice versa. After 1973, when Persian Gulf ports had excessive waiting times, the Volgo-Balt Canal was used by Soviet river boats for hauling cargo from Western Europe to Iranian ports on the Caspian Sea.

After the Revolution, Leningrad had served as a key industrial research and development center, especially for machine tools and heavy machinery. Although still important in these industries, other production centers have been established elsewhere in the Soviet Union, particularly after the Second World War, which has reduced Leningrad's relative position.

The Three Baltic Republics (Balticum)

The three small Baltic republics, Lithuania, Latvia, and Estonia, which had been part of the Russian Empire, enjoying a certain amount of autonomy, declared their independence after the October Revolution in 1917. They maintained their independence between World War I and World War II, throughout the interwar period. But in the Hitler-Stalin-Pact of 23 August 1939, they were accepted by Germany to be within the Soviet sphere of influence.[22] In 1940 they were occupied by the Soviet Union.

The new state boundaries after 1917 had deprived the ports in Balticum of much of their hinterlands formed in the second half of the last century with the opening of vast steppe areas in Russia to grain production and the construction of railroads. This had led to large exports of wheat and rye to northwestern Europe through the ports of the Baltic. In the interwar period this trade largely disappeared from the Baltic ports because grain surpluses for exports were reduced in the Soviet Union and what remained was routed by way of Black Sea ports. The national exports of the Baltic republics were primarily based on dairy farming.

Soviet initiatives for non-aggression pacts were first declined by the states of the "cordon sanitaire", wary of Soviet intentions. But Britain and France had little to offer as counterweights. Estonia in 1924, the year of an aborted Communist coup, invited Britain to send a fleet into the Baltic without success. In 1927 the British Secretary for Foreign Affairs declined to guarantee the status of Balticum. In 1929 the Soviet Foreign Secretary Litvinov finally succeeded in signing limited pacts with the Baltic republics.

Estonia

Beginning in the twelfth century the country was Christianized with archbishops at Bremen and Lund. Tallinn was founded in 1219 as a castle town by

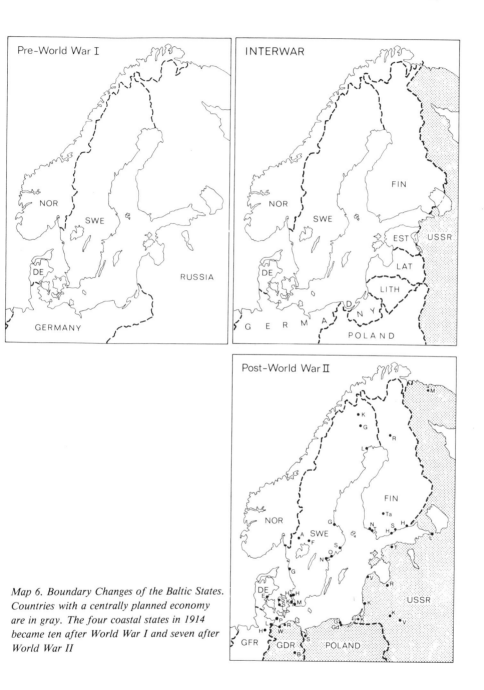

Map 6. Boundary Changes of the Baltic States. Countries with a centrally planned economy are in gray. The four coastal states in 1914 became ten after World War I and seven after World War II

the Danish King Waldemar II and soon joined the Hanseatic League. The Catholic Church was supported by the German Sword Brother Order, later by the Teutonic Knights. In the following centuries there were many uprisings by farmers against the German-Danish domination. In order to protect their country from Russian intrusions, the Estonian nobility in 1561 asked for Swedish protection. Estonia remained under Swedish sovereignty to 1721 when by the Treaty of Nystad it passed to Russia.

Latvia

East Baltic tribes in the ninth century moved into a territory thinly settled by Estonians. The inner parts of the present Soviet Republic came under influence of the Eastern Slavs and the coastal areas were dominated by the Danes and Swedes. In the thirteenth century the Teutonic Knights established a controlling German influence in the area. Around 1600 the Protestant Germany nobility and merchants, who dominated the towns although the peasants in the countryside were Latvians, sought Swedish protection against the catholic counter-reformation, led from Poland. Latvia remained divided between Sweden and Poland, with Riga in the Swedish part, until the Treaty of Nystad in 1721 and the third partition of Poland in 1795, when the whole country came under Russian rule.

Latvia declared its independence at the end of 1918. After more than a year of military intervention, with foreign volunteers, primarily from Germany, on the side of the national government, a new declaration of independence was written in 1920, which was acknowledged by the Soviet Union in the same year.

Lithuania

The Lithuanians came to their present territory in the beginning of the ninth century from the upper Oka and Volga River areas, from where they had been pushed by the Russians. Faced by attacks by the Teutonic Order, the Lithuanian groups were united about 1240. During the period of weakness that followed the Mongolian invasion of the Russian principalities, Lithuania occupied parts of White Russia and the Ukraine.

In the fourteenth century, Lithuania was an important power in Europe. New attacks by the Teutonic Order were repulsed and more Russian territory conquered, including Kiev, the center of the Ukraine and the ancient Russian heartland. A Polish-Lithuanian army won a decisive battle over the Teutonic Order at Tannenberg in 1410.

Under pressure from Russian forces in the east, Poland and Lithuania in 1386 entered into a dynastic union after which the fate of Lithuania was closely tied to that of Poland, especially after 1569 when Poland gained supremacy within a real union.

Balticum after 1940

The three Baltic republics Estonia, Latvia, and Lithuania, experienced strong russification after the Soviet occupation 15-17 June 1940. The Russian-speaking population makes up over 25 percent of the total people in Latvia and Estonia and almost 10 percent in Lithuania. The shares are even higher in the capital cities, especially Riga and Tallin, where they may be as high as 50 percent. Many new industries, working for the national Soviet market, have been established in Balticum as a result of a Soviet policy to integrate the region into the national economy. This has contributed to the Russification process.

The only regional raw material base of importance, in addition to agriculture, forestry, and fishing, are the exceptionally oil-rich shale deposits at Kokhtla-Yarve straddling the border between the Estonian and Russian Republics, with most of the production on the Estonian side. They long provided Leningrad and Tallin with gas, but the completion of pipelines to Leningrad from vast interior natural gas fields has reversed the flow. The large Baltic thermal power station (1.6 million kW) at Narva is based on oil shale fuel.

The Soviet petroleum industry expanded rapidly in the late 1950s. By the mid-1970's the Soviet Union was in first place among oil producers and in second place, after the United States, among natural gas countries. This development has also benefited Balticum. The Dashava power station between Vilnius and Kaunas in Lithuania (1.2 million kW) burns natural gas. These and other power stations are connected to form the north-western power grid that serves not only Balticum, White Russia, and adjacent parts of the Russian Republic up to Lakes Ladoga and Onega, but is suffucent also for exports of electricity to Poland. The large Soviet exports of petroleum to the other Socialist countries move by pipeline and transmission lines over the land borders (oil, natural gas, electricity). Exports to the hard-currency countries of the West have had high priority in all Socialist countries since the late 1960's.

Imports of machinery and advanced technology from the West, needed for the modernization process, can only be paid for by exports or credits. Both have been tried on a large scale with a rapid increase in East-West trade as a result. Among Soviet exports only raw materials are really competitive in Western markets, primarily oil and forest products but also coal. Natural gas is also exported to the West but only through extensions of the two trunk pipes that serve the Socialist countries of central ("eastern") Europe. Ventspils and other oil terminals on the Baltic (Klaipeda, Liepaya, Riga) are smaller than those on the Black Sea. Their combined capacity is some 30 million tons a year, of which Ventspils alone has 20 million. This terminal is connected with the Friendship (Druzhba) Line by a branch from Unecha. Coaking coal is shipped through Leningrad, Klaipeda, Riga, and Tallinn.

German East Prussia, which had never been under Russian control, was divided into Soviet and Polish occupation zones at Potsdam 1945. The northern, Soviet part includes Königsberg, renamed Kaliningrad, a medieval city which traditionally ranked among the major cities and ports on the Baltic with a hinterland stretching far into Russia. Kaliningrad Oblast, now an enclave of the vast Russian Republic, saw the repatriation of almost all its Germans and a replacement by Russians. The operation left the area with only about half its former population. No tendency of sustained immigration can be observed to this westernmost area of the Soviet Union on the Baltic which would be of great strategic importance were it not for the system of buffer states within the Warsaw Pact which extends the area under Soviet military control to the gates of Lübeck.

The port of Kaliningrad, located near the mouth of the Pregel River, has an outport of Baltiysk (Pillau) on the entrance of the Haff, which is the headquarters of the Soviet Baltic fleet. Other naval bases are at Leningrad, Tallinn, Riga, and Liepaya. In the modern transport system, river ports like Kaliningrad and Riga are at a disadvantage compared with ports directly on the sea, like Klaipeda and Ventspils, which are closer to the depths required by the large tonnage of today. The Baltic region is estimated by the CIA to have some 25% higher GNP per capita than the average for the USSR but only half that of Sweden and Denmark.

Poland

Poland has its origin in the tenth century when Duke Mieszko I, leader of one of the West Slavic tribes pushed westward but was defeated by Emperor Otto the Great. Mieszko in 963 accepted German supremacy and converted to Christianity. Lasting cultural and political links were thus established with central and western Europe (the Holy Roman Empire) and religious links with Rome, while the other Slavic groups were oriented towards Asia and the Byzantine Church.[23]

Great Poland *(Polonia Major)*, the oldest part of the country, was centered on the middle Warta River where the first Polish bishop was established at Poznan in 968. Little Poland *(Polonia Minor)* was on the upper Vistula River with Cracow as its capital. For a short period around A.D. 1000 Poland was a Great Power in Europe. After a long period of weakness Poland again played a prominent role in the fourteenth century when a dynastic union was established with Lithuania in 1386. The union eventually stretched from the Baltic to the Black Sea. In 1410 the influence of the Teutonic Knights was reduced through a decisive Polish victory in the battle of Tannenberg, and by the Treaty of Torun (1466) the mouth of the Vistula River, including the city of Gdańsk (Danzig), became Polish.[24] Victory in a long war with Prussia and the incorporation of a Polish shore front on the Baltic came at about the same time as Lithuania was losing its land on the Black Sea to an expanding Turkish Empire. Poland's position as a European isthmus state stretching from the Baltic to the Black Sea was of short duration.

The Polish kings had always been elective in theory although the incumbent prince was often chosen under the Jagiello dynasty, which became extinct in 1572 after almost two hundred years in power. Rivalry among Polish families prevented the establishment of a native dynasty and foreign princes were often elected.[25] Sigismund III, grandson of Gustav Vasa and cousin of Gustavus Adolphus, for a short time was also king of Sweden. After his deposition (1599) by his Swedish subjects, Sigismund[26] continued to push his claims, starting a series of Polish-Swedish wars, and in the 1650s Charles X of Sweden overran the country.

After a golden age from 1492 to 1648, the end of the Thirty Years War, Poland virtually ceased to be an independent country. Its fate was determined by three neighboring great powers: Russia, Prussia, and Austria. Through three successive partitions, the last one in 1795, Poland disappeared from the map of Europe.

In the years of national degradation a new spirit began to make itself felt which was of great importance for the future development of the nation. Napoleon in the Treaty of Tilsit 1807 created a Polish buffer state, the Grand Duchy of Warsaw, but it did not survive Napoleon's empire. The Congress of Vienna in 1815 set up an independent kingdom in personal union with Russia under the Tsar. Under the influence of the July Revolution of 1830 in France a general insurrection led to initial successes by a Polish army, but it was defeated by Russian forces, the constitution suspended, and a Russian governor general appointed to run the country. In 1863 a new revolt broke out in Russian Poland but the Poles were routed. Congress Poland in the following decades was run under a tight rein, officially referred to as "the Vistula area" and not the kingdom of Poland. A strong Russification program was inaugurated. A similar Germanization policy got under way in Prussian Poland. Only in Austrian Galicia did the Poles enjoy a considerable degree of autonomy.

The war of 1914-1918 gave Poland an opportunity to recover its independence.[27] Polish legions first fought on the side of Austria and Germany against Russia. In the United States, President Wilson in a message to the Senate in January 1917 spoke in favor of a united, independent, and autonomous Poland. Then the Poles in France near the end of the war raised an army and fought on the Western Front against Germany. In the Treaty of Versailles the Polish-Prussian borders of 1772 were more of less exactly restored. Poland got a corridor to the Baltic and Gdańsk was made a free city under control of the League of Nations.

On the eastern frontier, unsettled in the Treaty of Versailles, to which

Bolshevik Russia was not a party, the Poles demanded a restoration of the eighteenth century border, which included nearly all the Ukraine and White Russia. The Western powers proposed the "Curzon Line" several hundred kilometers to the west, fairly close to the linguistic frontier, which was muddled. The landlords in the borderlands tended to be Poles and the peasants Ukrainians. The Polish government refused to accept the Curzon Line and in April 1920 attacked the Soviet Union.

In the east, the Bolshevik army was first pushed back far into the Ukraine, but then advanced to near Warsaw before being stopped and pushed back again by the timely arrival of French military aid. By the peace treaty of Riga in March 1921, the border was drawn along the line at which military operations had come to an end, but neither Poland nor Russia recognized this frontier as final. Nor was Germany prepared to accept its own eastern boundary. The interwar position of Poland, with a double threat to its existence from its neighbors to the east and to the west, eventually precipitated the Second World War.

In the 1920's the Polish land borders were barriers to trade since Poland had strained diplomatic and economic relations with the Soviet Union, Germany, Czechoslovakia, and Lithuania. Economic geography makes Poland a great transit country for east-west trade on the North European Plain but in the 1920s the political geography of the nation hampered such development. Instead, many political factors worked in favor of a north-south or Baltic orientation of Poland's foreign trade. The Free City of Gdańsk was in customs union with Poland and the Poles were guaranteed an influence in the port and on transport matters of the city.[28] Polish-speaking people made up the majority in the Corridor. Not entirely satisfied with the trade and transport arrangements in the Corridor, the Poles built a new port on Polish territory at Gdynia just north of Gdańsk, primarily designed for coal exports

The coal fields of Upper Silesia have thicker and more homogeneous seams than competing fields in Europe. The favorable geology leads to larger production per man/day and lower production costs. Polish coal in the interwar years made heavy inroads on the traditional markets of British and German coal in the Nordic countries. British coal for the Nordic market came from fields in the northeast (Northumberland-Durham) near the coast. In spite of low pit-head costs, Polish coal could compete in Baltic ports with coal from Newcastle and Ruhr areas only because the long railway haul to Gdańsk-Gdynia was subsidized. At times, the export prices were set so low that Polish coal in Baltic ports was cheaper than in Poland.

In 1932 Poland signed a non-agression pact with the Soviet Union and in 1934 with Germany. When Germany at Munich in 1938 obtained a green light from Britain and France for the *Anschluss* of the Sudetenland of Czechoslovakia, Poland immediately sent Prague an ultimatum and occupied the

Teschen-area of Silesia with its coal fields and partly Polish population. The following year Germany demanded Danzig and a motorway through the Corridor. But the Poles in March 1939 had obtained British guarantees and refused Hitler's demands. At dawn, 1 September 1939, German troops launched an all out attack across the Polish border, and on 17 September Soviet troops entered Poland from the east, to the line agreed upon in the Hitler-Stalin Pact of 23 August. The Second World War started and Poland, "the monstrosity created by the Treaty of Versailles" (Molotov) had ceased to exist.[29] Throughout its history Poland has been a nation of drastically shifting borders. Slavic and Germanic tribes in this part of Europe were mixed in a crazy quilt pattern. Interwar Poland was no homogeneous national state either, in spite of the principles laid down at Versailles for drawing European borders according to the wish of the national majorities in the mixed areas. According to the 1931 census the Poles made up 60 percent of the population (35 million), the Ukrainians and White Russians in the eastern vojevodships 17 percent, the Jews 9 percent, the Germans 2 percent, and other minorities, mainly Lithuanians, 3 percent.

The 1945 Yalta-decision by the United States, Great Britain, and the Soviet Union to accept the Curzon line as Poland's eastern border meant a loss of 176,000 km^2 in comparison with the interwar period. Vilnius and L'vov were among the ceded cities. More than a million Poles were repatriated by the Soviet Union in exchange for 400,000 Ukrainians. The Polish loss of land was compensated by 100,000 km^2 of German territory in the north and west placed under Polish administration by the 1945 Potsdam Agreement. The land in the west, bordered by the Oder and Neisse Rivers, had been under Polish control in early medieval times but had been German for hundreds of years. Thus Poland was moved 194 km to the west. The German areas under Polish administration before the war had eight million inhabitants, but one million stayed and became Polish citizens.

Poland's dominating sea terminals are the twin ports of Gdańsk (Danzig) and Gdynia, west of the mouth of the Vistula in the Gulf of Gdańsk, and Szczecin, better known as Stettin, at the mouth of the Oder. The two port areas are about equidistant from the coal mining and heavy industrial district of Gorny Śląsk (Upper Silesia) and handle roughly equal shares of Poland's seaborne coal exports. The reserves in this coal field are estimated to be of the same order as those in the German Ruhr and considerably larger than those of the Soviet Donbass. Poland ranks after the United States but ahead of Australia and West Germany among the largest coal exporters in the world. In 1975, some 24 million tons of coal of a total of 50 million exported were shipped through the three ports.

The large Polish steel industry, dominated by the works at Nova Huta, just east of Cracow, imports most of its iron ore by rail from Krivoi Rog in the Ukraine and some by ship, primarily by way of Szczecin.

All of Poland falls within the Baltic drainage basin which, measured by population, makes it the most important Baltic nation. But the two leading manufacturing districts, in Gorny Śląsk and Warsaw, are far away from the coast. Traditionally, east-west land transports are more important than shipping in Poland's foreign trade. The high priority given to trade with the West in the recent five-year plans of all Comecon countries is likely to improve the position of Poland's Baltic coast as an industrial district. It is expected to pass Warsaw in industrial output and take second instead of third position.

Poland's Baltic coast, 139 km before World War II, was extended to 507 km after that war. Most of the coast is flat and sandy and not conducive to seafaring. Coastal currents, part of the anticlockwise general circulation, have straightened the shore, enclosed some lagoons, and built long sandspits, such as the Hel Peninsula north of Gdynia.

Germany

The first German city on the Baltic, Lübeck, was founded in the early twelfth century when the Germans went over the Elbe River and colonized the Slavic territory south of the Baltic, founding a number of principalities. All over northern Europe, including the Baltic region, German merchants and craftsmen made up a major sector of the urban entrepreneurs. German peasants colonized the countryside east of the Elbe, although they did not move as far from their home areas as the merchants. Often Germanic and Slavic villages were intermingled in the same area. In 1226 the Teutonic Order was called upon by one of the Mazovian Dukes to help against the pagan Prussians. The crusade was so "successful" that the Prussians, a Lettic people related to the present Latvians, disappeared.[30]

The Holy Roman Emperor gave the area to the Teutonic Order, whose *Hochmeister* took up residence in Marienburg on the Vistula. The monk-knights also subjugated Pomerania on the lower Vistula, a Christian country, and massacred the people of Gdańsk (1308). At Tannenberg (1410) the troops of the Teutonic Order faced not only the Poles and Lithuanians but also the Hanseatic cities of Prussia and were defeated. In 1465 the Teutonic Order had to accept the sovereignty of the Polish king. When Albrecht of Hohenzollern in 1525 became Hochmeister of the Order, he reorganized its territory into the Duchy of Prussia. Upon the extinction of his line in 1618, Prussia was merged with Brandenburg under Kurfurst John Sigismund, whose descendants ruled a gradually enlarged and evermore powerful state that became the German Empire in 1871. The defeat of Germany in 1918 in World War I ended the dynasty.

After the brief Weimar Republic of Germany during the 1920s, Adolf Hitler came to dictatorial power in 1933. He attempted to create a mighty Third Reich, including the Rhineland demilitarized in World War I, all of Austria and parts of Czechoslovakia and Poland, only to be disastrously defeated by a coalition of the Western Allies and the Soviet Union in 1945.

After World War II the remaining German core area, after Polish and Soviet occupations in the east, was split into two parts, separated by the "Iron Curtain", which in 1961, with the construction of the Berlin Wall, became the most distinct political boundary in Europe, more distinct than in 1945 when Winston Churchill had coined the term. Two states were created: the Federal Republic of Germany (FRG) or West Germany merged the three western occupation zones while the German Democratic Republic (GDR) or East Germany was formed in the Soviet zone. Berlin, the former German capital was first divided into four occupation zones. The Soviet zone in East Berlin became the capital of East Germany, and the three western zones were merged into West Berlin, a West German enclave within East Germany.

The nineteenth century had been the period of European colonial empires, the settling of North America, and expanding overseas trade, which emphasized the west coast of Germany and turned the Baltic into something of a backwater. With its late unification in 1871, Germany never became an important colonial empire, although not lacking in ambition. Instead of sending out its best young men to run rather primitive societies overseas, Germany and the Nordic states kept their elite at home, building business empires and organizing their own country. Whereas the trade patterns of Great Britain and France, not to mention the Soviet Union, have strongly reflected past or present political domination, Germany has had the most evenly distributed foreign trade of all the major trading nations.

The creation of the German Democratic Republic in 1949 in the Soviet zone of occupation marked the final arrangement of states within the Soviet sphere of influence in Central Europe. By nature, Germany was a land of four rivers: Rhine, Weser, Elbe, and Oder. Only the Oder empties into the Baltic. With the loss of Eastern Pomerania and Silesia to Poland, the Oder and its tributary, the Neisse, became the border of East Germany. The border makes a detour around Stettin, the port city of the Oder River. This port, closest to Berlin, now is the leading port of Poland. If the south-northerly Neisse-Oder is seen as the main river, all major tributaries come from the east, from present Poland. Almost all of East Germany falls within the drainage basin of the Elbe. However, the only coast of East Germany is on the Baltic. But it is a coast without any major prewar ports. Faced with this situation, East Germany has given high priority to the development of a national port in Rostock. This old Hanseatic city in the inter-war period was in the traffic shadow of Stettin and Lübeck on the Baltic and Hamburg on the Elbe.

The Iron Curtain has created more serious socio-economic problems than other frontiers in Europe. From the Baltic to the Italian border, the frontier divides mutually supportive regions in language, religion, culture, agriculture, industry and transport.

West Germany's short coast on the Baltic, between Lübeck and Flensburg, is the major crossroads for Baltic traffic. The geography of the Baltic region easily suggested that the neck of the Jutland Peninsula could be an interesting alternative to the Baltic straits for traffic between the "East Sea" and the "West Sea". Several combinations were tried before the construction of the Kiel Canal at the end of the nineteenth century, starting with the portage route of the Danish Vikings at Haithabu (Schleswig), the Stecknitz Canal built in the late 14th century, and the 18th century Eider Canal, only three meters deep. The Kiel Canal established Hamburg as a major transit port for the Baltic region in keen competition with Copenhagen and definitely reduced the importance of Lübeck.

The 99 km Kiel Canal, which allows ships of 10,000 gross tons and of eight meters draft, handles more vessels to and from the Baltic than the Sound. It shortens the distance between the Baltic and the Strait of Dover by some 300 miles. The canal has locks at both ends, 330 meters long, 45 meters wide and 14 meters deep. It is 102 meters wide at the surface, 44 meters at the bottom and 11 meters deep, with a 42 meter clearance under five bridges. The canal is being widened to 62 meters. In the mid-1970's the number of vessels entering or leaving the Canal excceded 60,000 a year, more than in any other canal in the world, while the corresponding number for the Sound was some 30,000 tallied at the southern entrance and 40,000 at the northern entrance. The IMCO-regulated transit route for large vessels passes through the Fehmarn Belt. The Great Belt handles some 20,000 ships and the Little Belt some 10,000 in and out passages. In terms of estimated cargo movements the relations are different. The Kiel Canal handles over 50 million tons a year, but the straits carry some 125-150 million tons, primarily through the Great Belt.

Travemünde, the outport of Lübeck, and Puttgarden (on Fehmarn) serve as the major Continental terminals of Nordic ferry lines. Puttgarden is on the fast rail and road connections between Copenhagen and Hamburg, which is served by ferry between Rødby on Lolland and Puttgarden, while Travemünde is the terminal for long-distance ferries from various ports in the Nordic countries. To avoid time-consuming border passages across the "Iron-Curtain", landfalls for the Nordic ferries are concentrated to the western Travemünde shore since the eastern shore is in East Germany. The old rail-ferry lines Trelleborg - Sassnitz and Gedser - Warnemünde and the new car ferry between Ystad and Szczecin primarily serve traffic between the Nordic countries and Central Europe. A contributing reason for the concentration of Nordic ferry lines to Travemünde (and Kiel) is the superior system of highways in the West European hinterland, compared to that of Central Europe, and the more streamlined border passages in the west.

Denmark

Ancient Denmark was made up of three "countries": Skåneland, with Skåne, Halland, Blekinge and Bornholm; Sjaelland, with adjacent islands to the south; and Jutland, with Fyn. The legislative assemblies *(landsting)* met at Lund, Ringsted and Viborg. The "countries" were rather loosely associated, with the king as the unifying element. The king was elected but was always chosen from the royal family. The first documented royal couple in Denmark were Gorm and Tyra, who reigned in the 940s and were buried at Jellinge near Vejle. Their son and his kingdom were converted to Christianity. When Denmark emerged in history as a united realm, all three straits leading into the Baltic lay within its boundaries. They were referred to as "the Danish Straits".

Danish and Norwegian Vikings went westward. For two or three centuries, when trade in Europe was at an ebb, the Vikings were both major agents of long-distance trade and regarded as a scourge by the settlements on the Continent and in the British Isles. The Norwegians colonized the Scottish Isles, the Faeroes, Iceland, and Greenland. Norse kings reigned in Scotland, on the west coast of England, and on the east and south coast of Ireland. They briefly established a small colony in Newfoundland (the Vinland of the Vikings). The Danes gained control over much of England northeast of a line between the estuaries of the Thames and the Dee (the Danelaw); and raided Spain and the Mediterranean coasts.

The major western tidewater port was Ribe. For the east-west trade, the portage between Schleswig and Hollingsted, some 15 km, offered an attractive alternative to the long and treacherous detour around the tip of the Jutland Peninsula, Skagen (the Skaw). Hedeby (Haithabu) at present-day Schleswig early became the leading trade center for the Vikings in the Baltic region in their trade with the Frisian merchants. The Danish king started to build a defense wall along the portage route between Hedeby and Hollingsted, the Danevirke, when Charlemagne around A.D. 800 had subjugated the pagan Saxons along the lower Elbe River.

After A.D. 1100 German colonizers on a broad front pushed eastward from the Elbe River. Within a relatively short time they founded a long string of cities from Wismar and Rostock in the west to Danzig and Riga in the east. Lübeck, founded in 1143, soon eclipsed Schleswig as a trading center. Denmark became a supplier of agricultural products to these coastal cities. Sea transport was simpler than overland hauls, which favored Danish peasants with their extremely good access to the sea. In Gotland, the traditional trading base of the Baltic, Visby, emerged as the walled emporium.

Danish kings in the 12th and 13th century extended the influence of their country widely in the Baltic region. Wendish pirates from their homeland on the south Baltic coast had been a serious threat to the coastal settlements in Denmark and southern Sweden, but their power was eclipsed when the Danes conquered Arkona on Rügen in 1169. A small remnant of the Slavic Wends or Sorbs can still be found south of Berlin, but the largest group are the Serbs in Yugoslavia. A peak in the Danish influence in the Baltic region was reached with King Valdemar the Victor and his Crusade to Estonia in 1219, where he founded Tallinn (Reval) as a fortress town. Throughout the medieval period Denmark was the strongest nation in the North and the leading competitor of the Hansa for trade in the Baltic area. By 1530 Denmark had superseded the Hansa as the leading power in the Baltic and remained in that position for a hundred years.

Denmark's Nordic dominance was reflected by the population size. In the twelfth century Denmark was estimated to have had over one million people, Sweden had some 600,000, and Norway about 400,000. The Norwegians had been very active during the Viking period but more or less dropped out of European history at the end of the middle ages. The reason seems to have been that Norway was hit harder than other European countries by the Black Death in 1349-1350 when one-third of her population was lost. Norway did not recover from this blow until the early sixteenth century.

A development of great importance to the Hanseatic League and to the nutrition of much of northern Europe were the large herring fisheries in the southern part of the Sound. Skanör became a trade center on a par with Ribe. Tens of thousands of people met at the Skåne markets in the fall to buy and sell herring. The Lübeck merchants brought salt that had been mined at Lüneburg for the herring. The herring trade gave rise to new cities that soon were to outshine Skanör, primarily Copenhagen and Malmö. Copenhagen with its excellent harbor, protected by Absalon's Castle, was near the crossroads of the land route between Ribe and Skanör and the sail route through the Sound, the shortest distance between the East Sea (the Baltic) an the West Sea (the North Sea).[31]

Until sail yielded to steam in the 1890's,[32] the Baltic countries were the main providers of naval timber and stores to western Europe, primarily to the Netherlands and Britain. At the same time, Russia and her Baltic provinces were the main suppliers of naval stores (hemp and flax for cordage and sail cloth, pitch and tar), especially to the British navy and merchant marine, which were completely dependent on Russian hemp and flax. Two Baltic countries, Sweden and Russia, dominated world exports of bar iron, for which Great Britain was the leading market. Charcoal-based bar iron was versatile in use and was preferred to coke-melted iron far into the second half of the 19th century. All Russian and most of the Swedish bar iron was shipped through Baltic ports. In short, Britain was deeply involved with Russian and other Baltic trade, so that the fear of a closure of the Sound by Denmark, backed by Russia and France, was a major reason for the two British attacks on Copenhagen (1801, 1807). British fleets had sailed into the Baltic repeatedly in the 18th century and during the Napoleonic wars. In 1808, the British and Russians fought a navy battle in the Sound; during the Crimean War they fought again at the Åland islands; and in 1919 the British again engaged Russian naval forces on a limited scale. At the beginning of World War I, after a Danish declaration of neutrality, Germany asked the Danish government if it planned to mine the Great Belt against the two belligerent parties. It was understood that Germany otherwise would mine these waters and place batteries on Danish territory to protect the minefields. No objections were raised by the British against the Danish compliance with the German request.

The Treaty of Versailles (1919) provided the border between Denmark and Germany should be redrawn on the basis of a plebiscite to be held in the following year. The outcome was that the northern part of Schleswig returned to Denmark while the rest, including the city of Flensburg, remained in Germany. The two duchies, Schleswig and Holstein, on the narrow base of the Jutland Peninsula, had been closely associated with each other and with Denmark since prehistoric times. Through long association with German Holstein, Danish Sleswig had been Germanized in its southern part. In the war of 1864 the two German Great Powers, Prussia and Austria, radically pushed back the Danish border not only north of German Holstein but north of the Danish speaking part of Schleswig as well.

Denmark acts as an island bridge between the Scandinavian Peninsula and the Continent. No point in this archipelagic realm with a coast line of 7,400 km is more than 52 km from the coast. Its only land border, with Germany, is 68 km.

Agriculture has always played an important role in the economy of Denmark, one of the most fertile and densely cultivated countries in Europe, has 61 percent of the land area under the plow, which should be compared with 7 percent in Sweden and 8 in Finland. But the old standardbearers of Danish exports, butter and bacon, have run into saturated markets and nonprofitable prices. Meat and fish have emerged as other leading Danish export products but most conspicuous is the growing importance of the engineering industry as an earner of foreign currency. Denmark's economy has become more diversified. Manufacturing and the service industries, not the least transportation and wholesale trade, are important activities in the small NATO and EEC country controlling three approaches of the Baltic, the Great and the Little Belts and the Sound.

Copenhagen over the centuries had developed a flourishing transit trade and eventually became the largest city on the Baltic. It first competed with Lübeck, the headquarters of the group of trading centers in northern Europe known as the Hanseatic league, and in the last decades of the nineteenth century it was challenged for size by St. Petersburg. Its transit trade was diminished by Hamburg, which, at the tidewater end of the Kiel Canal, became, a formidable competitor. In 1980 about one fourth of the total Danish population lived in Copenhagen.

Boundaries and regional arrangements after 1945

The Second World War led to radical changes in the political boundaries of the Baltic region. At Potsdam in 1945 the Allied Powers had accepted the Oder-Neisse line as a *de facto* administrative boundary between Poland and Germany pending a final arrangement in a peace conference. But the peace conference was never held, Germany was divided into occupation zones, which led to the present Federal Republic of Germany (West Germany) and the German Democratic Republic (East Germany), with Berlin as a western enclave within East Germany.

A unilateral boundary change, moreover, occured when the Soviet Union occupied Estonia, Latvia, and Lithuania, transforming them into socialist republics under the sovereignty of the Soviet Union, although the legality of this transfer of sovereignty has not been acknowledged by several governments, including the United States.

The post-war boundary changes affected the shorelines of Germany, Poland, the Soviet Union, and to some extent Finland, all of which face the Baltic Sea,[33] and raised particular questions about the extension of coastal state jurisdiction over the adjacent waters for navigation, resource exploitation, and marine pollution, which will be discussed later.

During the Cold War period between the United States and the Soviet Union from 1948 to 1955, West Germany, Denmark, and Norway stood with the West against Eastern Germany and Poland in the Baltic area, while Finland, which had signed a defense and friendship pact with the Soviet Union in 1948, did not join the Soviet Union's Warsaw Pact, a counter to the western North Atlantic Treaty Organization (NATO). Sweden proclaimed its continuing policy of non-alignment in peace and neutrality in war.

Norway differed from the other two North Atlantic Treaty states, West Germany and Denmark, in the region by not being a littoral state of the Baltic. Although it has a coast on the Skagerrak, and thus a direct strategic interest in the Baltic region, it has not been included in this study. However, a realistic discussion of the Soviet Union and the Baltic Sea cannot be separated from the Soviet naval installations in the Kola Peninsula and the vital importance of Murmansk as a Soviet gateway to the world ocean. The tacit Norwegian recognition of the Kola coastline as the location of the main naval base of the Soviet Union and the Russian refusal to tolerate a hostile offensive weaponry nearby, has been expressed in Norway's conditions for being a member of NATO: no nuclear weapons nor foreign troops can be stationed on Norwegian soil, and no NATO exercises can take place within 300 km of the Soviet border.

The Nordic Council and Nordek

Nordic cooperation since the end of World War II has made greater strides than at any similar period in history. At the beginning of the Cold War (1948-1949) the Scandinavian countries had started negotiations for a defense alliance, but Norway and Sweden could not agree. The Norwegians favored military support from the United States; Sweden favored a non-aligned alliance. The split was evidently a result of different experiences during World War II, and there were differing opinions about the capability of Sweden's manufacturing industry to supply the whole of Scandinavia with armaments, including planes and tanks. In that situation, first Norway and then Denmark decided to join NATO in 1949 on condition that foreign bases and nuclear weapons would not be placed on their territories.

Finland took no part in these Nordic negotiations; the Finns had already signed their friendship and mutual assistance pact with the Soviet Union in 1948. Both Sweden and Finland claimed a policy of neutrality. The Swedish version has usually been stated as "non-alignment in peace and neutrality in war". The Finnish has been stated as "mutual assistance pact in peace aiming at neutrality in war". The Swedish non-alignment and the restrictions in the NATO-engagement of Norway and Denmark have at least partly been motivated by a desire to facilitate Finland's relations with the Soviet Union, to make Norden a stable and peaceful part of Europe, "the Nordic balance". Sweden in the late 1940s had declared (a) that she considered the other Nordic countries capable of formulating their own security policy and (b) that Sweden's security was so closely tied to that of Finland that any substantial change in the position of the old "half of the realm" might lead to reorientation of Sweden's security policy (the "Erlander Doctrine").

The Nordic Council, formed in 1951, is a Nordic "parliament" that meets for almost a week every year. Members are appointed by the national parliaments and by the governments. The number appointed by the parliaments are fixed: 16 from each of the four large coutries and five from Iceland. Åland appoints one and the Faeroes two, but these delegations are included in those of Finland and Denmark. The number of participating ministers from each country varies. The Council does not make any decisions, only recommendations. Important work has been done in the five committees dealing with legal, cultural, social, transportation, and economic problems. Since 1971 the Council has maintained a permanent office in Stockholm.

In February, 1968, the Danish Prime Minister H. Baunsgaard suggested an economic union, Nordek, which got the unanimous support of the Nordic Council. Several meetings of the Nordic prime ministers were held in the first half of 1969. Nordek would simplify for the four countries (Iceland was not participating in the negociations) the participation in or cooperation with a widened European Economic Community (EEC). The proposed Nordek cooperation was not to be in conflict with existing agreements. Foreign and security policy would be outside the scope of Nordek. Advantages and disadvantages for the four countries should balance. The agreement would be valid for ten years at a time with an option for Iceland to join. If one country became a member of the EEC, the agreement could immediately be suspended.

In April 1970, President Kekkonen declared that Finland would not join Nordek; the negotiations then speedily came to a standstill. The possibilities for a widened EEC had in the meantime brightened. Denmark and Norway appeared interested in joining.

The postwar attempts at a Nordic economic union, however, foundered on the option of a wider market cooperation, in 1959 within the European Free Trade Association (EFTA) and in 1970 within the EEC. Both Denmark and Norway put in applications for membership in the EEC; however, the plebiscite that preceded the final decision was positive in Denmark but negative in Norway. Thus Denmark became one of the EEC-9 in 1973 while the other three countries signed free trade agreements. To the split in security policy, therefore, which took place in 1948-1949 came the economic split of 1970-1973. However, Nordic economic, social, and cultural cooperation has continued unabated.

A summary of the most important achievements of Nordic postwar cooperation would include the following: a common labor market in 1954, followed in 1955 by a social security convention that gives a Nordic citizen the same advantages in other Nordic countries as those enjoyed by the local citizens. In 1957, Norden became one passport area. A cultural agreement was signed in 1972 and one covering transportation and communications in 1973. A Nordic environmental protection convention dates from 1974.

In addition to official cooperation, numerous private groups and associations work closely with their counterparts in the other countries. But most striking is the transformation of Norden to one home market, as seen by business firms in the five countries. All products, from nails to prefabricated houses, are exportable. For example, Norway and Denmark in recent years have ranked after West Germany and Britain and Finland has been just ahead of the United States among the trading partners of Sweden.

European Free Trade Association (EFTA)

A Nordic customs union was suggested by Norway in 1947 and negotiations were carried on over the years, with the participation of Finland after 1956. In 1959 events in the rest of Europe made the idea obsolete, or rather, the geographic frame too narrow, for the plans for the European Free Trade Association (EFTA) made the Nordic solution less attractive. EFTA was formed in May 1960, and a year later Finland joined as an associate member.

In Britain, EFTA was seen primarily as a stepping stone to the European Economic Community (EEC). Already in 1961 Britain had put in an application for membership. Denmark followed, but Norway and Sweden waited. Later Norway asked for membership and Sweden for associated status. Finland did not approach the EEC. The different reactions in the four capitals was predictable and reflected how the four countries saw their geopolitical situation in a wider context than that of Norden.

EFTA turned out to be much more successful and longlived than expected at its start. Trade between the Nordic countries has registered remarkably rapid increases and Norden has become a home market for all five countries. Between 1959 and 1967 exports to other Nordic countries increased twice as fast as exports to all destinations, and in multilateral negotiations for trade with western Europe and the United States, the Nordic countries have had a common chief negotiator.

Comecon and the Warsaw Pact.

Although invited to join in the American Marshall Plan for the rehabilitation of Europe after World War II, the Soviet Union refused, fearful of the Plan as an effort to recover the capitalist system and undermine Soviet hegemony over Eastern Europe. In 1949, therefore, Moscow launched the Soviet equivalent of the Marshall Plan, namely, Comecon, although foreign economic aid had not been part of Soviet ideology. Indeed, few benefits went to the eastern satellite states, for the Soviet Union not only exacted war reparations from them, but also set up a number of companies in these subjugated states as joint ventures with Moscow as a partner. As economic conditions worsened, threats of revolt or actual revolt occurred in East Berlin, Hungary, Czechoslovakia, Romania and Poland. The Russians, therefore, cancelled the remaining war reparations, dissolved many of the joint companies, and tried to integrate the trade of the Eastern European states with its own. Some of the tension was released, but some economic independence was achieved by the Eastern European states. Whereas in the 1960s about 70 percent of all their trade had been within the Soviet bloc, in the mid-1970s only about 60% was entirely within the Soviet bloc.

The Soviet Union also reacted to the formation of the North Atlantic Treaty Organization in the West by creating the Warsaw Pact in 1955. Using a formal treaty, indicating equality among partners, the Soviet Union refurbished the military forces of the allied Eastern European states, but command clearly remained in the hands of Moscow. For the Soviet Union, the Baltic is one of several important seas. For the Warsaw Pact it is *the* important sea. But the strength of the Pact lies primarily in the landbased forces, for in a narrow sea, like the Baltic, large navy vessels are at a disadvantage since many airfields and land-to-sea missile ramps are within close range. Conventional sea battles were not fought during the two world wars within the Baltic Sea itself and can hardly be foreseen in the future. More on this subject will be presented in Chapter 4.

Chapter 4

THE BALTIC STRAITS

The Baltic Straits include the Little Belt, the Great Belt, and the Sound, as shown in Map 7. The Sound traditionally was the shortest and busiest passage between the Baltic Sea and the Kattegat, but with the increasing size of ships the Great Belt has become the most frequently used route for the passage of large vessels. Smaller ships still may choose the Sound or reach the North Sea through the Kiel Canal. The Kiel Canal and the Sound are busiest in numbers of passages, but the Great Belt accounts for the largest tonnages transported.

The Samsøe Belt, the Great Belt, the Fehmarn Belt, and the Kadet Channel for all practical purposes form one seaway for large vessels entering or leaving the Baltic. This route is regulated by traffic separation lanes established by the Intergovernmental Maritime Consultative Agency (IMCO) at critical stretches as shown in Map 8.[1] From a legal point of view, assuming a 12-mile territorial sea, this route would be divided into two international straits by a triangular area of six square miles in the Mecklenburg Bay: that is, coming from the north, a ship would pass through the Samsøe Belt, the Great Belt, and the Fehmarn Belt, then the triangular area of high seas, then the Cadet Channel.

Various risks of international complications may cause some Baltic coastal states to refrain from claiming the full breadth of 12 mile for their territorial sea in the narrow Baltic approaches. For example, Sweden on 1 July 1979 widened its claim from the traditional four miles to twelve miles, but in December 1979, after consultation with Denmark, Stockholm declared that it withdrew its claim to three miles from the midline in the Kattegat and in the new international strait at Bornholm. With the reduced claims of both countries, a six-mile channel of exclusive economic zones exists in the Kattegat and at Bornholm. The main approach in the Kattegat to the Baltic Straits measured less than 24 miles between the Swedish baseline and the Danish line (the islands of Laesø, Anholt and Hesselø). A withdrawal of claims to leave a six-mile channel centered on the midline has prevented therefore the creation of a new international strait in the Kattegat (and at Bornholm).

For the shipping industry, a "compound strait" like the T-Route, established by the Danish government, is functional, although it comprises straits with varying legal regimes, from the Great Belt, which is an international strait through the Danish territorial sea, to the Kattegat and the Kadet

64

Map 7. The Baltic Straits Orientation Map

Channel, which will remain routes through exclusive economic zones.

The Little Belt between Jutland-Als and Fyn-Aerø is delimited in the north by a line from Aebelø to Bjørnsknude, 9.7 km long, and in the south by a line from Pøls-Puk to Vejsnes Nakke, 23.3 km long.[2] The width of the Belt varies between 700 meters and 27.5 km. Islands divide it into channels of which the ones most used for navigation are Aarø Sund between the Jutland coast and Aarø, with a channel of 350 meters between the six meter contours, and the much wider Baagø Sund between Fyen and Baagø. The northern approach to the Little Belt is through internal waters between Fyn and the two islands of Samsøe and Endelave.

The current is strong in the Belt, up to three meters per second, and unpredictable. "Eddies" are formed. Depths increase from about 17 meters in the northern part to as much as 81 meters in the narrow section and then again decrease to as little as 15 meters in the southern portion. The threshold depth is 13 meters in the Little Belt. With the opening of the Little Belt bridge on 15 May 1935, passage was limited to ships with a mast height of no more than 33 meters.

The Great Belt between Fyen-Langeland and Sjaelland-Lolland is delimited in the north by a line from Fyns Hoved to Røsnes, 22.2 km long, and in the south by a line from Gulstav Flak to Kappel Church, 18.5 km long. It is separated from the Smaaland Sea between Sjaelland and Lolland by a line 22 km long. The area between this line and Langeland is usually called the Langeland Belt.

The width of the Belt varies between 18.5 and 28.2 km. At Sprogø it is divided into two channels of about equal width, the West Channel between Knudshoved and Sprogø and the East Channel between Sprogø and Halsskov. The navigable channel in the West Channel is about 3.3 km wide and in the East Channel 1.7 km. Between the reefs outside Agersø and Vengeance Grund the channel between the 10 meter contours is only 1.8 km. Through traffic is separated at Sprogø and moves in the East Channel. A bridge over this channel must be high enough to allow the tallest ships to pass without delay between Sprogø and Halsskov, but a bridge across the West Channel could be lower.

Currents are rather stable in the Great Belt. The outgoing surface current of brackish Baltic water travels at a speed of up to 1.5 meters per second. Depths vary from 20 to 25 meters in the northern part of the Belt to 66 meters in the southern, allowing even the largest ships that can enter the Baltic to pass through this Belt.

To ensure the safety of navigation and reduce the risk of oil pollution from collision or grounding of tankers the Danish Government has established a transit route, "Route T", from Skagen (the Skaw)[3] to a point northeast of Gedser with a minimum depth of 17 meters, as shown in Map 8. The route is marked by lights and has a good Decca coverage. Portable Decca equipment

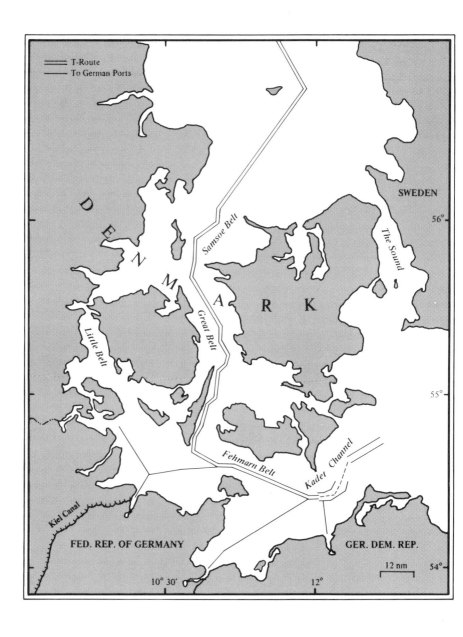

Map 8. Route T through the Great Belt

are available for hire at the pilot stations of Skagen and Allinge (Bornholm). Danish icebreakers render free assistance when needed. A radio reporting service informs large ships of the position of one another to avoid meeting in narrow waters or sharp bends. It also notifies the ferries crossing the Belt south of Sprogø about the passage of large ships. Heavy traffic here moves in the East Channel, which has traffic separation lanes. Traffic is also separated in the Kadet Channel through the Darss Threshold. The Intergovernmental Maritime Consultative Organization (IMCO) has recommended that ships of 40,000 deadweight tons (dwt) or more or with a draft of 13 meters or more fulfill certain conditions about equipment, when navigating through Route T. A detailed description of Route T and navigation rules are available from the Danish Administration of Navigation and Hydrography in Copenhagen.

Route T was made necessary by the rapid increase in ship size after the mid-1950s. T-2 tankers from World War II had been the typical oil carriers, with a capacity of 16,200 dwt and a draft of 9.2 meters. By 1967 the average capacity of 134 tankers on order had increased to 208,000 dwt with a draft of 18.3 meters, which meant that the average new tanker of the early 1970s could no longer enter the Baltic. A T-2 tanker at full speed (15.5 knots) was able to come to a "crash stop" in five minutes after having covered 0.9 km. The largest tankers that can enter the Baltic, some 150,000 dwt, require 15 minutes and 3.9 km for a crash stop.

In shallow water, defined as less than 1.5 times the draft of the vessel, the maneuvering properties of large tankers change perceptibly. Two other factors must also be taken into consideration: first, the chartered depths may be reduced by as much as two meters due to unknown and moving obstructions; two, the vessel's draft may be increased by more than one meter at full speed because of the "squat" of a ship in the water. A reduction of speed from fifteen to four or five knots is therefore required in areas of shallow water.[4] The compelling conclusion is that the safe operation of large tankers requires special navigational privileges in international straits, especially where the cross traffic is heavy, such as south of Sprogø in the Great Belt and in the Fehmarn Belt.

The Sound or Øresund between Sjaelland and Skåne has a northern limit at Gilbjaerg Hoved - Kullen (21.9 km) and a southern at Stevns light - Falsterbo Point (24.7 km). The width varies between four km (Helsingør - Helsingborg), where the Sound Dues were once collected and where now the railway ferries between Denmark and Sweden move, and 47 km at Køge - Klagshamn. The distance between København and Malmö is 29 km. The Sound is divided into an eastern and a western channel by the island of Ven. The eastern channel continues near the Swedish coast through the threshold south of Malmö.

The western channel, 8.3 km wide, moving southward is divided into two channels, which unite again between Amager and Saltholm and leads into the wide southern part of the Sound. Kongedyb has a 650-meter wide navigable channel, Hollaenderdyb about 850 meters and Drogden at its narrowest point only about 250 meters while Flintrännan is about 450 meters.

Large ships can enter the harbors of Copenhagen and Malmö from the north, but the depth south of this line is insufficient for modern shipping. In the five-km wide water between Copenhagen (Amager) and Saltholm the depth is five meters or less, except for a one to two km zone at the ship channel from Copenhagen, the Drogden, where it approaches 10 meters. Between Saltholm and Limhamn the depth is mostly six to seven meters, except at the Flint Channel, the main shipping channel on the Swedish side, where the depth is some nine meters. The official depths at medium water listed for the Drogden is 7.7 meters (6.2 to 6.9 meters before being dredged) and for the Flint Channel 7.5 meters. Some traffic moves in two smaller channels, the Saltholm Channel, east of Saltholm, and the Trindel Channel, near the Swedish coast. The threshold in the southern part of the Sound is a flat bedrock of limestone covered by limy mud and sand with a thickness of up to two meters. Between Saltholm and Copenhagen the soil cover on top of the limestone reaches a thickness of 10 meters.

To facilitate cabotage a 7.2 meter deep canal was completed in 1941 across the neck or "tombolo" that connects the north-southerly Falsterbo sandspit with the mainland. The Falsterbo Canal continues to the north with a seven-km dredged channel in the direction of Flintrännan. The sandspit extends submerged for miles to the north and especially to the south (Falsterborev) with depths of one to two meters. In the 1940s over 10,000 vessels of up to 2,500 net register tons passed the Falsterbo Canal every year but in recent years the number has dropped to a little over 4,000. In addition, 10,000 vessels of 20 net registered tons or less have been transiting the canal, most of them pleasure boats.

Measured by tonnage flows, the Great Belt is displacing the Sound as a passage. But the traffic volume in the Sound is large enough to warrant IMCO traffic separation both in the north and the south. The cross traffic in the Baltic Straits is as important as the through traffic which makes for a very busy traffic region. Only the Little Belt has been bridged but advanced plans exist for bridging the Great Belt and the Sound. The ferry traffic in this part of the Baltic region has few counterparts, if any, elsewhere in the world.

From a transport agent's point of view, a ferry is a bridge. The main carrier in his door-to-door transport system is the truck or passenger car and the ferry is seen as a low-standard bridge that does not allow a continuous flow of traffic. The ferry, like the bridge, as a rule is placed where the sea distance is shortest. Inland, the rivers and fiords are crossed by ferries until the traffic volume warrants the construction of a bridge. A bridge across an international strait, however, must be built so as not to interfere with substantial, multi-national through traffic, which means not only very high construction costs, but when two coastal states are involved, like Sweden and Denmark, long and complex negotiations to solve both the sharing of the financial burdens and regional planning problems in wide areas around the bridge access routes.

The Åland Sea

The approaches of the Gulf of Bothnia in the Åland Sea on either side of the Åland Islands are also international straits. They are regulated by the Swedish and Finnish laws on the admittance of foreign navy ships and military aircraft to the territorial waters of the two countries. A treaty of 1921 on the demilitarization and neutralization of the Åland Islands, reiterating the Paris Treaty of 1856, explicitly stated that the prohibition for entrance and stay of navy vessels in the demilitarized zone should not interfere with their innocent passage through the territorial waters. Both countries have claimed the need for prior notification by such vessels, but Sweden has made an exception to this general claim in the Sound. In the South Quarken, the border between Sweden and Finland cuts across the small island of Märket and the deep channel into the Gulf of Bothnia thus is in Swedish territorial waters.

Kalmar Sound

The narrow waters between the island of Öland and the mainland north and south of Kalmar form an international strait much used in the past. With the increase in vessel size this traffic now primarily moves outside of Öland. The Kalmar Sound was bridged at Kalmar in 1972. Europe's longest bridge (6.07 km) is low from Öland to the sailing channel just off the harbor entrance at Kalmar where the clearance is 36 meters. The sailing channel is narrow here and a strong current makes navigation hazardous for larger vessels.

During World War II Swedish navy vessels convoyed merchant ships between Bergkvara, at the southern end of the Kalmar Sound, and Landsort, south of Stockholm. Larger vessels were convoyed outside the island through the Swedish mine fields off southeastern Öland. Among the vessels passing through the Sound were German troop transport vessels on their way to Finland. This was in agreement with international law as enunciated in 1923 in the Wimbledon Case with respect to the Kiel Canal.

Since the widening of the territorial sea to 12 miles by Sweden in 1979, a narrow slot of international water has been left between the two Swedish islands of Öland and Gotland.

The Sound Dues

For more than four centuries (1429-1857) the Danish government collected a transit duty on ships passing through the Sound. The duty was originally imposed by King Erik of Pomerania during a war with the Hansa. Protests from the Hanseatic League about the legality of the impost were met by the Danish kings with claims that the straits were Danish territory and that the Baltic Sea was a closed sea under Danish sovereignty.[5] However, ships from the various North German cities from Hamburg to Stralsund as well as those of Sweden and Denmark were exempt from the dues when sailing with their own cargo.

Originally the dues had been a ship duty, which was raised several times in the first hundred years. It was graded into four categories: ships in ballast or loaded and with more or less than a hundred lasts loading capacity. Later a load tariff was added, calibrated according to the size of the ship. In reality, it developed into a tariff duty. The dues reached their peak when Denmark succeeded Lübeck as the leading power on the Baltic about 1530, especially after the increases of 1567. The dues were collected at Helsingør, the narrowest part of the Sound, where the castle of Kronborg was built in the sixteenth century to replace an older castle that was contemporary with the introduction of the dues. All transits through the Belt were originally prohibited, but at the end of the fifteenth century it became possible to sail through the Great Belt and pay dues to the tax collector in the city of Nyborg. A special customs house was built there in 1560. Only domestic and local traffic was permitted, except for vessels from Lübeck and Rostock on their way to Denmark or Norway. Other ships were prohibited from sailing through the Belts, which carried only about 10 to 15 percent of the traffic.

The Sound dues at their peak contributed some two-thirds of the Danish state budget. The accounts provide the best source of information on the economic history of shipping in the Baltic, although they have to be used with great circumspection. Nowhere else has a comparable trade route been covered by such a long series of data. The passage of ships through the Sound can be traced 350 years back from 1857 and the flow of cargo has been recorded for 300 years.

According to the records, a non-littoral country, the Netherlands was the dominant shipping nation, accounting for between half and two-thirds of the ship passages in the Sound between 1500 and 1650. It remained the leading nation shipping through the Sound up to the nineteenth century, and the Dutch flag is still one of the most common in the Sound today, flown by many coasters plying the North Sea ports and the small ports of the Baltic.[6] In the early sixteenth century, a total of some 1,000 Sound passages a year by all ships were reported; in the 1630s some 3,400; and at the end of the eighteenth century they had increased to 7,000 a year. The two countries suffering most from the dues were the Netherlands, the leading shipping nation, and Sweden, whose imports were made more expensive. Although Swedish ships and goods were exempt from the dues, most of Sweden's international trade was carried by foreign vessels.

In 1640, when Sweden had overtaken Denmark as the leading power in the Baltic, Sweden and the Netherlands reached an agreement to promote the freedom of trade.[7] However, this did not mean that Sweden had become a champion of the freedom of the seas. Gustavus Adolphus in 1630 had claimed *dominium maris Baltici* for Sweden and he continued traditional Swedish strategy when, entering the Thirty Years War in the same year, he attacked the mouth of the Oder River. Most river mouths between Finland and the Oder were already under Swedish control: the Neva, the Narva, the Dyna, the Memel, and the Vistula. The customs duties from these strategic ports accounted for a substantial part of the Swedish budget. Dutch trading interests in the Baltic were particularly sensitive to Swedish control of the Baltic ports. Just as Holland earlier had worked to prevent Danish dominance in the Baltic, the Dutch in the mid-seventeenth century tried to hold in check Swedish expansion and threats to Dutch commercial interests in the Baltic Sea.

After their defeat in the war with Sweden from 1643 to 1645, the Danes were forced by the Treaty of Brömsebro leading to the Kristianopel Tariff of 1645 to reduce the dues from 25 to 80 percent, not only for Holland but also for Britain, France, and Hansa. The Kristianopel Tariff was not replaced until 1842, a few years before the Sound Dues were abolished.

By the Roskilde Treaty in 1658 Denmark ceded Skåne to Sweden and thereby put the Sound under joint Danish-Swedish control. Sweden had first tried to make Denmark "the guardian of the Baltic" with the task of keeping foreign warships out of the Baltic Sea. Failing this, Sweden itself secured the territorial base on the eastern shore to stop the passage of warships. Denmark was to be the "door keeper" of Sweden's "mare nostrum". Two years later Charles X Gustavus tried to take control also of the western shore of the Sound, but the death of the King and the intervention of both Holland and Great Britain stopped the attempt.

The Nystad Treaty after the Great Nordic War in 1721 established Russia as a great power on the Baltic Sea. Thereafter Russia made every effort to prevent the British vessels from sailing in the Baltic. An agreement between Denmark and Sweden in 1756 at the opening of the Seven Years War and another between Russia and Sweden of 1759 were unsuccessful attempts to keep British ships out of the Baltic. A Russo-Swedish fleet was to be stationed in Drogden, but Denmark protested while inducing England not to force the issue.

The Convention of the League of Armed Neutrality (1780-1783), concluded at Russian behest with Denmark and Sweden in 1780, to which Prussia and Austria acceded in 1782 and Portugal 1783, aimed to protect their commerce against British capture during the War of American Independence. In a convention of 1800 between Russia, Denmark, Sweden, and Prussia an attempt was made to renew the League in order to prevent the British navy from entering the Baltic, but this too, was unsuccessful. The British navy first battled in the roadsteads of Copenhagen in 1801. The bombardment of the capital, and the capture of the Danish fleet in 1807 forced Denmark to denounce the convention and realize that it could not prevent Britain from sailing on the high seas of the Baltic. Napoleon and Alexander I, the Tsar of Russia, at Tilsit in 1807 had agreed that Denmark should be "the guardian of the Baltic". Russian protests after the shelling of the Danish capital were met by British arguments that she had never accepted a closing of the Baltic to warships, which would be unneutral and contrary to international law.[8]

Beginning in the 1820s, criticism was voiced against the Sound dues not only by foreign governments but also by the merchants of Copenhagen. The dues were said to wreck the transit trade of the capital. One of the reasons for building the Göta Canal from 1810 to 1832 across Sweden from Söderköping to Lake Vänern, connecting the Göta River and Göteborg, was to avoid paying the Sound dues on the grain trade.[9]

But the Danish government was reluctant to abolish the dues, for they still contributed about one-eighth of all Danish revenues. The decisive event came in 1845 when the United States as a matter of principle declared that it would refuse to pay the Sound dues.

The Americans had challenged Denmark's right to levy the dues "under the public law of nations". Washington was not impressed by the antiquity of the dues:

> But the foundation of this claim were laid in a remote and barbarous age, even before the discovery of America; and the reasons which are now alleged in its support have no application whatever to the United States. They apply exclusively to the nations of Europe.[10]

In 1855 the United States decided to press the subject of the Sound dues to a conclusion. When Denmark sent out invitations to a conference on the Sound dues, the United States refused to take part unless the conference dealt explicitly with Denmark's right to levy the dues. Otherwise American participation might be construed to be a recognition of Denmark's right, which might create difficulties for American ships in other international straits. However, the United States indicated that it would pay its share of indemnities to Denmark if an agreement on discontinuing the dues could be reached.

In the Copenhagen Convention on the Sound and the Belts signed by the European shipping nations on 14 March 1857, Denmark obtained an indemnity corresponding to an annual income capitalized to the current value from the signatory states. As a result the dues were discontinued after 1857. The largest contributor to the indemnities was Great Britain, closely followed by Russia, each paying about a third of the total. This indicates that, as in the past, a non-littoral state had been the leading user of the straits. For hundreds of years it had been the Netherlands and in the nineteenth century it was Great Britain.

A special straits convention between the United States and Denmark was also signed in Washington in 1857. For a compensation of $393 million, Denmark allowed American ships free passage "in perpetuity". Since 1857 no other multilateral treaties or conventions have been concluded regarding the Baltic Straits. However, the Treaty of Versailles in Article 195 reiterated the right of "free passage into the Baltic to all nations".

The 1857 treaty has influenced the text of the Third UN Law of the Sea Conference's Draft Convention of 1980. An exception has been made to the regime for straits as set forth in the Draft Convention for those straits "in which passage is regulated in whole or in part by long-standing international conventions" (Art. 35c).

This was inserted to satisfy the Danish delegation. However, international lawyers seem to disagree about the existence of such a convention for the Baltic Straits. All agree that naval vessels were not covered by the 1857 treaty since they did not pay Sound Dues. Erik Brüel, after a detailed discussion of the treaty relating to the right of passage for merchant vessels, arrives at the opinion (International Straits, 1947):

Since the conclusion of the treaty, the right of passage of merchant vessels in time of peace... is subject to the general rules of international law dealing with the right of passage of such ships in international straits...

In a paper read at the 14th annual conference of the Law of the Sea Institute at Kiel in 1980, Wolfgang Graf Vitzthum drew the same conclusion as Erik Brüel that there was no special regime for merchant vessels in peace-time in the Baltic Straits. But Ib Andreasen at the same meeting claimed the existence of a special regime, arguing that Denmark would not be in a position to levy future hypothetical dues if such were instituted by the United Nations in all international straits because of the 1857 treaty.

The 1857 treaty thus could be seen as one of the longstanding international conventions referred to in Article 35c of the Draft Convention (Informal Text).

The Baltic Straits (1857-1945)

According to the neutrality rules laid down by Denmark and Sweden-Norway, on 5 January 1854, prior to the outbreak of the Crimean War, the three countries declared that they would allow all harbors except a few naval bases to remain open to warships of any belligerent powers. The rule also applied to their territorial waters and the Straits. None of the major powers protested, and Denmark was under strong pressure at that time to abolish the Sound Dues, with negotiations already started. In February Great Britain tried to get Denmark to close the Sound and the port of Copenhagen to warships on the ground that the Russian fleet, which did not draw as much water as the British Fleet, could sail up the Sound at the same time as the British fleet sailed down the Belt and thus cut off their retreat.[11] Denmark replied that its guns at Kronborg did not reach ships keeping close to the Swedish shore and that it was thus not in a position to close the Sound. London then gave assurances that it would respect Denmark's independence.

A British fleet of 16 battleships and frigates driven by paddle-wheels and screws under Admiral Sir Charles Napier on 26 March sailed south through the Great Belt and was later joined by a French squadron. The British fleet sailed all the way to Kronstadt off St. Petersburg, near Peterhof where the Tsar and his family were in residence. But the Russian navy would not come out to fight and Napier felt incapable of attacking it in the harbor.[12] Great Britain and France thereafter confined themselves to assaulting and destroying certain island fortifications at the approaches to St. Petersburg, primarily Bomarsund in the Åland Islands. A subsidiary operation tried to destroy the stocks of naval stores, principally tar and pitch, at Finnish ports.[13] Although a direct naval assault upon the Russian fleet in the Baltic had been avoided, another danger remained. Russia feared a major Allied landing, which would have been joined by Sweden, and for the rest of the war Russia kept 200,000 of her best troops, including the regiments of the Imperial Guard, in Finland and around St. Petersburg. The British-French blockade of the Russian coast was only partially successful, and the naval campaigns of 1854 and 1855 were cut short by the first autumn frost. The severity of the Baltic winter was legendary, and the main theater of the war became the Black Sea and Crimea. The relatively meager results from the strenuous Baltic effort probably influenced British naval thinking in later wars,[14] for it demonstrated that a Baltic power was in a strong position against foreign marine troops operating far from their bases.

After the Treaty of Vienna (1864), by which Prussia obtained Schleswig-Holstein, a third coastal state appeared on the Baltic Straits. Prussia, soon to be the unifying state of Germany, held the western shore of the Little Belt from the middle of Hejelsminde Bay to the southern end of the Belt. The acquisition of Schleswig-Holstein made it possible for Prussia to move her Baltic navy station from Danzig to Kiel in 1865, a complement to her North Sea navy base at Wilhelmshaven built after 1854, and for Germany to build the Kiel Canal from 1887 to 1895. The canal was of great strategic importance, allowing the rapid movement of the German Baltic fleet to the North Sea and vice versa. During these years Denmark more and more came within the German sphere of influence.

During the Franco-Prussian War from 1870 to 1871 the straits were again left open under rules similar to those of the previous war. French ships sailed into the Baltic through the Belt. In the Russo-Japanese War from 1904 to 1905 the straits were open and Danish pilots were permitted to pilot the warships. On 19 October 1904, the ill-fated Baltic Fleet of Russia sailed north through the Great Belt. Although Japan did not protest this passage, it objected to the fleet being piloted by Danish state pilots.

Before the outbreak of World War I no special rules existed regulating the passage of warships through the Baltic straits except the Danish claim that prior notification must be given when passing through the Hollander Deep and Drogden and the assertion of Denmark's right to close these channels. The general rules of international law relating to the passage of warships in international straits remained in force.

In the Anglo-German naval rivalry after the turn of the twentieth century, the British started to build 18,000 ton "Dreadnoughts", the first of which was commissioned in 1906, to outstrip the enlarged German Fleet. The first vessel in a series of German dreadnoughts, the 19,000-ton *Nassau,* was launched in Kiel in 1909. Ships of this size could not pass through the Kiel Canal. Germany deepened the canal, completing the work in 1914 and enabling even the largest warships at that time to transit from the North Sea to the Baltic and vice versa. Great Britain concentrated a large part of its fleet in the North Sea, the "Home Fleet". The theory was that Britain had to have a fleet twice as large as Germany in the North Sea in order to shut up and blockade the German North Sea Coast. The German Admiralty believed that an Anglo-German war would start with a British attack on Kiel, similar to Japan's strike at Port Arthur in 1904, a fear that was increased by the British interest in the Baltic and in Denmark in the years preceding World War I. The British fleet visited the Baltic in 1905.

According to the Danish defense plan of 1909 the Hollander Deep and Drogden would be closed in the event of war by mines to protect the roadsteads of Copenhagen, which were defined as Danish internal waters. On 2 August 1914, as World War I began, the mines were laid, and through traffic was directed to the Danish part of Flinterenden.[15] Meanwhile the Commander at Kiel had been informed by the German Admiralty that the British navy might attempt to break through to the Baltic on the night of the second of August. The Admiralty and the Commander acted independently of each other. The former asked Denmark to close the Great Belt against both belligerents; the latter ordered German ships to lay mines in the southern outlet of the Great Belt. German mines were also laid in Aarø Sound in the Little Belt, but these were in German territorial water.

The German government wanted to respect Danish neutrality and not drive Denmark into the arms of the enemy. However, British control of the Danish Islands and the Baltic Straits was to be avoided at all costs. In response to the German request for the closing of the Great Belt and the news about German mine-laying in the southern end of the Langeland Belt, the Danish foreign minister told the German ambassador that Denmark would close the Great Belt with mines as well as the Danish channel in the Little Belt and the Sound. The minister also notified the British minister who replied that the Danish mine-laying seemed a "quite reasonable" step. At the same time in the evening the German ambassador conveyed his government's regrets to Denmark that mines had been laid in the southern part of the Great Belt. Mine-laying in the Great Belt started on 6 August 1914 and was completed on 14 August, after which sailing instructions were sent out. Merchant vessels could pass through the minefields in daylight with pilots. Flinterenden and the German channel in the Little Belt was left open, and it was intended to keep all the Baltic Straits open for merchant vessels.

The only infringement on Danish neutrality during World War I occured when a German destroyer fired on a British submarine in Danish territorial waters in Flinterenden on 19 August 1914. The channel there had not been closed and a few British submarines passed through this channel during the war. Merchant traffic through the Great Belt was quite heavy. Some 32 thousand vessels were piloted during the war through the minefields in the Great Belt. The straits were cleared of mines immediately after the armistice of 11 November 1918.

Sweden considered itself a neutral state in World War I and did not close its international waterway, Flintrännan, to the warships of the belligerent powers. The German navy was instructed to avoid infringing upon Swedish territorial waters as far as possible. Thus, Sweden maintained the same neutral status as Denmark without mining its international channel. In fact, the denial of the Baltic Straits during World War I only applied to large warships, for smaller ones could use the Flintrännan. Moreover, the minefields were hardly seen as an effective resistance to a deliberate British attack[16] when Great Britain was "on the search for a naval offensive," hesitating between a strike through the Baltic Straits or through the Dardanelles at the Black Sea, the mines were only considered a delaying factor. An attack through the straits, planned for June 1916, was thwarted by the Battle of Jutland on 31 May 1916.[17] Germany also reversed her view on the value of the mines in the course of the war, for they were gradually seen as a hindrance to the German use of the Kattegat as an exit to the North Sea and the full use of the strategic advantage provided by the Kiel Canal. The Russians did not protest to Denmark about the mine-laying, but Petrograd repeatedly tried to persuade Great Britain to attack in the Baltic, which meant that the government did not consider the mines a serious tactical impediment.

Sweden laid mines in her territorial waters in the Sound; i.e., in the Kogrund Channel between the land and the Bredgrund shoals off the Falsterbo spit. This channel had not been normally used by shipping that sailed out to international waters, but the channel had been dredged to serve Swedish cabotage. When Britain and France began to bring back vessels, which had been laid up in the Baltic, through this channel, it was closed with mines to other than Swedish vessels in July 1916. The reason was fear that Germany might be tempted to violate Swedish neutrality. To answer protests by London and Paris, Sweden pointed out that the Kogrund Channel was a purely domestic channel, normally without importance to international shipping. It had only acquired a temporary importance as a result of unlawful acts of other powers, which could not influence Sweden's right to mine the channel.

After the First World War, Germany and the Soviet Union, the two major states on the Baltic Sea, were weak and disorganized. There was no question of closing the Baltic Sea to the victorious powers. Britain sent a fleet into Baltic waters immediately after the armistice to establish the principle of *mare liberum*. Britain supported the three small republics in Balticum while France supplied Poland. The Kiel Canal was given the status of an international canal in the Versailles Treaty. It was to be "free and open to the vessels of commerce and of war of all nations at peace with Germany". German artillery positions between the Danish-German border and east of the Oder, which could threaten shipping through the Baltic approaches were dismantled. The status of the Kiel Canal came before the International Court of Justice at the Hague in 1923. The *Wimbledon*, a British vessel chartered by a French company and carrying munitions for the Polish government, had been refused passage by Germany and had lost 13 days making the detour through the Baltic Straits. The Court decided against Germany, holding that the Kiel Canal was open to states at peace with Germany if such states were engaged in a war in which Germany was neutral. In the opinion of the Court, the Kiel Canal, since the Versailles peace treaty, fell in the same category as international straits in the sense that "even the passage of a belligerent man-of-war" did not compromise the neutrality of the riparian state.[18] In 1936 Germany unilaterally denounced the relevant articles of the Versailles peace treaty. The Kiel Canal returned to its pre-1919 status as German interior waters as most of the interested signatories of the treaty did not protest this breach of international law. After 1936 the Kiel Canal, although a waterway of great importance to international commerce, had the same legal regime as the other canal-outlet from the Baltic Sea, the Soviet White Sea Canal, which was completed in 1933, a purely domestic waterway that is closed by ice 200 days every year, that can only handle vessels up to a five-meter draft, up to 115 meters in length, and up to 3,000 gross tons. In the absence of a peace treaty between West Germany and the Allied Powers after World War II, the legal status of the Kiel Canal remains unclear.

The new Soviet Union, created by revolution in 1917, continued the traditional, Russian policy of trying to make the Baltic a *mare clausum,* which Moscow hoped to dominate after the defeat of Germany in World War I. The Finnish peace treaty of 1920 thus contained a clause about the neutralization of the Baltic, while Soviet delegates at international conferences in Riga (1923) and Rome (1924) made proposals that the Baltic Sea should be closed to foreign warships. The decision of Denmark in 1923 to dredge the Drogden Channel in the Sound to eight meters was described in 1925 by *Izvestia,* the official newspaper of the Soviet government, as an attempt to facilitate Britain's access to the Baltic. Nor was the decision well received in Germany, very sensitive at that time to an attack on her Baltic coast. In war games of 1923-1924 the German navy command concentrated all large navy units in the western part of the Baltic against the enemy, a French fleet trying to establish connection with Poland. During the game the Germans tried to inflict heavy losses on the enemy already in the Baltic approaches, the Kattegat and the straits.[19]

In the late 1930s Denmark came under strong political pressure from Adolf Hitler's expansive Third Reich of Germany. Copenhagen had to sign a non-agression pact with Germany, and then was forced by Berlin in 1938 to accept an overflight clause for the three Baltic straits as well as a clause allowing submarines under pressing circumstances to pass submerged, that is, for all practical purposes allowing the submarine captain to decide how to transit. The Danish overflight clause met with very strong British protests, but Denmark under the prevailing rise of German power could do nothing to accommodate the British interests. Josef Stalin, like Peter the Great, as Russian dictator always had his interest focused on the Baltic approaches. In his 1939 negotiations with the western Allies that preceded the Ribbentrop Pact with Germany, he claimed a navy base in Jutland, and in 1940 the same claim was put to Hitler. In Teheran in 1943, he demanded of the western Allies a navy base in Denmark, and in Yalta in 1945 he told Winston Churchill and Franklin D. Roosevelt that he wanted a Kiel-Canal-Zone under Soviet protection. When the occupation zones were drawn up for Germany at the end of World War II he tried hard to have Fehmarn included in the Soviet zone. In all these instances the Soviet claims were rejected by the British.[20] The occupation of Bornholm by Soviet troops also came to nothing and they had to leave the island.

The Baltic Straits and Approaches since World War II

The Baltic Straits and their approaches have been of great strategic importance to both the Western Allies and the Soviet bloc in the post-World-War-II period. In 1962 the NATO forces in the area were reorganized for strategic reasons and formed into the Allied Forces Baltic Approaches Command (COMBALTAP),[21] with its subordinate navy forces, NAVBALTAP, and air forces, AIRBALTAP. The NAVBALTAP command has operated some 200 German and Danish units plus the German naval air force. One third of the staff has been Danish, one-third German, and one-third British, American, and Canadian. The command has alternated between Danish and German admirals. The area of responsibility of NAVBALTAP covers a 100-km wide stretch west of Schleswig-Holstein and Jutland, the southern half of the Skagerrak, the Kattegat, the Baltic Straits, and the Baltic Sea.

The main task of NAVBALTAP has been to prevent the Warsaw Pact (WP) forces from spilling out of the Baltic Sea, which would threaten Allied reinforcements in the North Sea during a military conflict. The WP forces are thus defined as offensive and the NATO forces as defensive. The structure of the WP naval forces confirms such an interpretation of the overruling strategy of the two power blocs.

The Soviet Baltic Fleet is one of four fleets of the Soviet Union, less important than the Northern Fleet based in Murmansk on the Barents Sea, with access to the Atlantic Ocean. But the Baltic ports, primarily Leningrad and Kaliningrad, are of great significance for building, repair, and maintenance of the fleets. The Baltic shipyards in recent years have built eight times as many naval units as the yards of the non-Baltic base-areas combined. Poland has rapidly expanded its capacity as a major shipbuilding and repairing country and some services are also available in the German Democratic Republic.

The modern core of the Soviet Baltic force is made up of 3,500 ton Krivak destroyers, Nanuchka missile-carrying corvettes, and a large number of missile-equipped Fast Attack Craft. The combined Soviet, Polish, and German Democratic Republic amphibious force in the Baltic represents some 40% of the total Soviet lift capacity. When the large merchant fleet of roll-on, roll-off vessels recently launched or under construction is added the lift capacity is expected to meet any Russian needs.[22] Additions to the Soviet amphibious capacity in 1980 were high-speed air-cushion vehicles, which were almost invulnerable to conventional mines. Thus, hit and run or small-force landings by Soviet forces may now be possible in places once considered inaccessible. Moreover, the transfer of Golf II submarines, conventionally propelled but carrying three ballistic missiles with a range of 1,200 km and a nuclear warhead from the Northern to the Baltic fleet has added a significantly increased threat to Central Europe. In 1980 the total of Warsaw Pact Naval

Forces was estimated as 25 missile and conventional destroyers; two conventional cruisers with many escorts; 250 minesweepers; 100 torpedo and 60 missile boats; and 70 submarines.

To the naval forces of the Warsaw Pact should be added the strong air forces at its disposal for use in the Baltic approaches. More than 700 aircraft have been based in the German Democratic Republic, Poland, and the western military districts of the Soviet Union. Some of these have been just a few minutes away from Denmark. The WP Baltic forces seem much stronger than any need for defensive purposes. The large amphibious capacity of the navy, for example, could only have an offensive role. The landing ships, among them the new Soviet Ropucha and East German Frosch types, have a capacity of 5,000 troops for the first wave of attack. The personnel strength of the WP amphibious forces in the Baltic in 1980 was about 10,000. These naval infantry units were very mobile, equipped for independent action in the initial phase of a landing. The merchant ships, cargo vessels, and ferries, could carry seven motorized divisions. The roll-on, roll-off vessels could land amphibious forces on an open beach while unloading of motorized follow-up forces would require port facilities or at least floating dock installations on the beach.

Just as NATO regularly flies signal intelligence flights in the southern Baltic and east of Gotland, called "streetcars" by Swedish fighter pilots on a TV-program referring to their fixed routes and schedules so the Soviet air force follows NATO telecommunications from signal planes and flies long range bombers in the direction of the Baltic approaches and back again, turning around at Rügen. Warsaw Pact navy vessels on training tours often circumnavigate the Danish islands through the Sound and the Belts.[23] Permanent patrol vessels from the Soviet bloc haven been stationed south of Falsterbo, east of Møns Klint, and northwest of Fehmarn for signal intelligence and radar control of traffic in and out of the Baltic,[24] Maritime suveillance seasonally has occurred east of the Skaw and frequently also at the Baltic entrance of the Kiel Canal. Radar stations on NATO, Warsaw Pact, and Swedish territories reveal great activity in the air and on the water in the Baltic Sea and its approaches. Not much goes undetected. A ship entering the Baltic area through the Skagerrak is followed by landbased Swedish radar through the Kattegat, the Sound, the Baltic proper and into the Gulf of Bothnia. Ships passing by either side of Gotland are followed and registered by a computer at Visby, jointly operated by the Swedish navy and coast guard. The NATO and Warsaw Pact electronic surveillance is not less intense. For the nuclear power balance, intelligence gathered by NATO planes, flying regularly over the Baltic between the island of Gotland and the Soviet Coast, is indispensable. Nowhere else is the high sea so close to the Soviet heartland.[25]

The Baltic Sea is also of great economic interest to many maritime states of the world. The Skagerrak has been listed among eleven straits of the world of "major economic significance" to the United States, along with the Florida, Dover, Hormuz, Mocambique, Gibraltar, Bab el Mandeb, Malacca, Lombok, Luzon, and Bosporus-Dardanelles straits.[26] On an average day 150 vessels enter or leave the Baltic Sea through the straits and the Kiel Canal. About one-third fly a Soviet bloc flag. Around 700 ships plus as many fishing vessels are at sea in the Baltic on an average day, and a total of over 200 ships a day pass on one side of Gotland or the other.

Legal Views of the Baltic Straits

The states of the Soviet bloc distinguish among straits according to geographic and trade criteria. They differentiate between: (a) those that connect two parts of the world ocean, are the "streets of world trade", and have global importance and (b) those that connect the world ocean with a closed sea, are of importance primarily to the littoral states, and give those states access to the world ocean. A German Democratic Republic textbook, *International Law,* lists the straits of Gibraltar, Magellan, Malacca, Dover, and Florida as examples of the former, and the Bosporus, the Dardanelles, the Sound, the Belts, and the straits of Tiran and Hormuz as instances of the latter.[27] The former are said to serve world trade, the latter are considered primarily of importance for the coastal states of these seas.

In modern Soviet literature only those straits that connect two parts of the world ocean are considered international straits. Approaches in those seas on which the Soviet Union is a littoral state (the Baltic Sea, the Black Sea, the Sea of Japan, and the Sea of Okhotsk) do not fall under the regime of international straits in the Soviet view. For these seas the Soviet Union suggests that the coastal states should agree on a regime that takes into consideration their trade and security interests in the respective sea. In fact, the three coastal states of the Soviet bloc on the Baltic have launched the idea of neutralizing the Baltic Sea, turning it into a "Sea of Peace".[28]

The argument for trade interests of the Soviet bloc is not as convincing as it may seem at first even if the legal concept of an "enclosed sea" were accepted. If trade should be measured by origins or destinations of trade flows, at least one littoral state of the enclosed sea would by definition be involved in all trade transactions. But this to a large extent may also be true for straits indisputably connecting two parts of the world ocean, such as the Magellan Straits, or for straits that could be listed as outlets of an "adjacent" sea, such as the Florida Straits, which lead to a sea that is enclosed in the view of the oceanographer. If instead the flags of the ships carrying the cargo are considered, which is a vital legal element of shipping, the situation is quite different. Non-littoral states have always played a prominent, sometimes a dominant, role in

82

the traffic through the Baltic Straits. Through and cross traffic in the Baltic Straits account for more international trade than some of the straits listed by the German Democratic Republic textbook as "open to ships of all flags in peace and war.".

Passage through the Baltic straits has been regulated through Swedish (3 June 1966) and Danish (27 February 1976) laws on the admittance of foreign naval ships and military aircraft to Swedish/Danish territory when each respective country is at peace.[29] Foreign naval ships are free to pass through the Swedish part of the Sound according to the rules of innocent passage: i.e., they must neither stop nor anchor, and submarines must move on the surface and show their flag. Foreign naval vessels are thus allowed to move through the southern part of the Sound in Swedish territorial waters in peace and war when Sweden is neutral without prior notification. Naval vessels of belligerent states must make their passage in less than 24 hours.

The Danish law makes a distinction between the traditional approaches to the Baltic, the Sound and the Great Belt, on the one hand, and the Little Belt on the other. The rules of innocent passage of naval vessels apply to the Sound and the Great Belt if the passage through the Sound does not involve the Copenhagen harbor parts of the Drogden and the Hollander Deep, which are claimed to be internal Danish waters. Passage of naval vessels through the Sound and the Great Belt or the Little Belt is allowed subject to advance notification through diplomatic channels. When more than three naval vessels of the same nationality plan to be simultaneously in the same part of the straits, permission from Danish authorities through diplomatic channels is required. Foreign submarines must under all circumstances move on the surface and show flag in Danish territorial waters. Foreign military aircraft may fly across Danish territory only after having obtained permission through diplomatic channels. Permission is granted only if an ordinary ICAO flight schedule has been submitted prior to the flight to the Danish traffic service agency and the flight follows the ICAO guidelines and provisions laid down by the Danish aeronautical authorities. Sweden does not require permission for overflight in the Sound.

In connection with the planning of bridges or tunnels across the Sound and the Great Belt, the international law experts of the Danish and Swedish ministries of foreign affairs have made statements about the obligations of the coastal states. The general principle of innocent passage for all vessels sailing through a strait connecting two parts of the open sea, which was confirmed by the 1949 decision of the International Court of Justice in the *Corfu Case*, is followed by Sweden.

Some commentators on international law have argued that the right of innocent passage of all vessels through straits refers to full passage. From this it would follow that vessels unable to pass through the shallow southern part of the Sound would not be in a position to claim the right to pass through the northern part. However, large vessels destined for Malmö or Copenhagen have to pass through the northern part of the Sound. Of course, Sweden could close Malmö and Denmark could close Copenhagen, thus preventing large vessels from entering the Sound from the north; but Sweden cannot prevent access to Copenhagen and Denmark cannot prevent access to Malmö, so that this interpretation of the general principle of innocent passage for the northern part of the Sound seems irrelevant.

Must all the three parallel Baltic Straits be kept open for all foreign warships if Denmark itself is not at war with their states? Denmark has an obvious security interest in closing the Drogden channel, which passes through areas defined as within the harbor area of the Danish capital and thus Denmark's internal waters. If the Sound must be kept open, Flintrännan could serve as the waterway closest to the midline and thus enhance the neutral interests of the two coastal nations of keeping passage through the Sound as far away from the coasts as possible. The narrow and winding nature of the Little Belt justifies the special requirement of notification through diplomatic channels of any such passage as set forth in the Danish ordinance.

A handbook for commanders of the Soviet Navy criticises the Danish ordinance for not taking into consideration important interests of the other littoral states of the Baltic Sea and denounces the exceptional rules for exercises by Naval vessels in the NATO states. In fact, the Swedish and Danish regulations on the use of the Baltic Straits are in agreement with international law, the Geneva Convention of 1958 on the Territorial Sea and the Contiguous Zone as well as customary law on the use of foreign territorial waters by navy ships.[30] The Soviet commentator, P.D. Barabolia does not question this but states that the regulations are in conflict with "an old tradition to acknowledge the special interests of the littoral states", which explains why the Soviet Union, Poland and the German Democratic Republic insist on the idea of neutralizing the Baltic Sea, turning it into a "Sea of Peace".

The Draft Convention (Informal Text) of 1980, which evolved from the negotiations of the Third UN Law of the Sea Conference that began in 1973, contains articles that, if applied to the Baltic Straits, would be in conflict with existing Swedish and Danish law. The Draft convention provides that in straits that are used for international navigation "all ships and aircraft enjoy the right of transit passage, which shall not be impeded". "Transit passage" is "freedom of navigation and overflight solely for the purpose of continuous and expeditious transit of the strait". However, the requirement of a continuous and expeditious transit does not preclude passage through the strait for the purpose of entering, leaving, or returning from a state bordering the strait, subject to the conditions of entry to that state. (Articles 37 and 38).

In contrast to the laws of the two states that use the "innocent passage" principle, the new international law would use "transit passage", which comes close to "free passage". Transit passage can neither be withdrawn nor limited. It includes overflight by planes as well as submerged transit by submarines, which are elements of the freedom of the high seas.

The widening of the breadth of the territorial sea from the traditional three miles to twelve miles is another innovation in the Draft Convention, but this is one of the least controversial issues in the Draft Convention. The Soviet Union has claimed 12 miles since the 1920s; Tsarist Russia had made similar claims. Other Baltic states have widened their claims to 12 miles under the influence of the Law of the Sea negotiations: Poland on 1 January 1978 and Sweden on 1 July 1979. But for the coastal states of the Baltic approaches the application of a 12-mile territorial sea would cause various problems, which explains why up to 1981 Denmark, the Federal Republic and the German Democratic Republic have hesitated to expand their territorial sea.

Although Sweden had widened her territorial sea from four to twelve miles on 1 July 1979, five months later, after consulting with Denmark, she decided to withdraw to three miles from the midline in the new international straits that would be formed by the maximum claims of Sweden and Denmark. The debate in the Swedish Riksdag on 18 December 1979 reveals some of the arguments for and against the change in the claims. With maximum claims to a territorial sea by both Sweden and Denmark, the Kattegat, an area south of the Sound at Falsterbo, and the Hammer Gap at Bornholm would all become international straits. Under the Draft Convention on the Law of the Sea foreign naval vessels and military aircraft would be allowed transit passage through and over these waters. Thus there would be virtually free movements by foreign naval vessels as well as overflights by foreign military aircraft between the Swedish and Danish base lines. Warships and military aircraft flying a foreign flag would have the right to move just outside the Swedish coast without previous notification[31] as long as they fulfilled the qualification for making a transit passage. Therefore, many Swedish legislators felt that a withdrawal to three miles from the midline would leave Sweden with up to nine miles of territorial sea adjacent to the six-mile slot or high seas.

The arguments in the Riksdag against pulling back the claims were the same as those for widening the territorial sea: first, better possiblities for protection of the coast against pollution from merchant vessels, primarily oil spills. In the debate reference was made to an instance when planes of the Coast Guard had spotted a ship spilling oil but had no authority to interfere since the act was occuring on international waters. A wider territorial sea, second, would make military activities by foreign states more difficult. An instance not mentioned but relevant are the Soviet permanent patrol vessels at Falsterbo, Møn, and Fehmarn which would have to be moved out.[32] Third, it was argued that the Draft Convention may never be ratified. Many coastal states on international straits, among them Sweden, have argued against the "transit passage" concept and continued to favor "innocent passage". The United States and the Soviet Union, the two superpowers have been the main proponents of transit passage in international straits. The superpowers, of course, have sought to maintain their own strategic interests by a system of legal obligations in the straits of the world that would not limit the mobility of their naval forces.[33]

The Swedish-Danish agreement on the narrow waters lying between them could become a precedent for other parts of the Baltic approaches and perhaps for other international straits of the world. It will not affect the traditional Baltic Straits, which predominantly lie within Danish and Swedish territorial seas, even with claims of only three miles by Denmark in 1980 and only four miles by Sweden up to 1979.

Denmark is expected to widen her claims to a territorial sea to 12 miles on the west coast. But in the Baltic approaches the situation is complex. If Denmark and the German Democratic Republic should widen their territorial sea to 12 miles the Kadet Channel would become an international strait. The two busy ports of West Germany, Kiel and Travemünde (Lübeck), would have no direct access to the open sea. East Germany would face another serious problem: If all states in the area should widen their territorial sea to 12 miles, the distance for refugees fleeing into another state by sea would be shortened by up to nine miles. "Hot pursuit" of refugees is allowed, according to international law on the high seas, but not on a foreign territorial sea, which would be nine miles closer to the point of the refugee's departure from the shore.

Laws about the security and protection of the coastal areas of the German Democratic Republic of 21 June and 10 July 1962 provide for a five-km border zone on the mainland within which all individuals have been checked.[34] The "Border Brigade Coast" of the People's Navy, established in 1962, has been charged with the task of preventing citizens of the country from fleeing across the Baltic. In spite of these measures, more refugees leave East Germany over the Baltic than over the land border.[35] To protect itself the German Democratic Republic does not allow innocent passage by naval or merchant vessels through its territorial sea without explicit permission. This rule is not in agreement with Article 14 of the 1958 Geneva Convention on The Territorial Sea and the Contiguous Zone, which was ratified by the German Democratic Republic in 1974 nor does it follow customary international law. Some communist countries, when ratifying the convention,[36] have made a reservation against the innocent passage of naval vessels, which, according to

Article 14 requires "notification" through diplomatic channels but not permission, thus creating a different legal interpretation of the convention by the communist states. This creates no problems in the Baltic approaches as long as the German Democratic Republic claims a three-mile territorial sea, but it would become a serious problem if it widened its claim to 12 miles since the Kadet Channel is eight miles from the East German shore. If this part of the Baltic approaches became an international strait, foreign naval vessels and military aircraft would be entitled to innocent passage anywhere between the Danish and East German base lines. Neither Denmark nor the German Democratic Republic, therefore, are likely to make maximum claims for a territorial sea in this part of the Baltic in the near future. The interests of both the coastal states and the international community may be served best by adapting territorial sea claims to local conditions and not by automatically making the maximum claim of 12 miles.

Closing the Baltic Straits

A final consideration about the political, economic, and legal status of the Baltic Straits as international water highways is the possibility of turning the straits into "terra firma" by the construction of dams at their entrances. Such construction work would be of the same magnitude as the construction of breakwaters in harbors like Genoa.[37] The reclaiming of land on this scale has been demonstrated in the Netherlands. Farm land on both sides of the three straits are among the best in Europe; the area is densely settled and new land would soon find many urban uses, not the least for highways across the isthmus to the continent. But could it be done?

Erik Brüel, in dealing with the 1857 Sound Treaty, raised this question, asking whether Denmark had undertaken any obligations to keep the navigable waterways open: to dredge, to break ice, or to force a blockade by another power? He answered in the negative.[38] The treaty assumed that the straits were navigable waterways, but did not impose on Denmark any duty to maintain them as such. But they cannot remain navigable waterways if Denmark (and Sweden) take active steps to deprive them of their character as straits. Did the treaty assume that all three straits would be kept open or could one or two be closed as long as one international strait is left? Brüel's conclusion was that one strait would be sufficient as long as it was the one that could accomodate all ships that might enter the Baltic Sea. The Sound has serious depth restraints on ships and the Little Belt, since the opening of the bridge in 1935, has vessel height limits. Drying out the Sound, which would facilitate important vehicle cross traffic, would not seriously inconvenience the through vessel traffic.

Since the 1857 Treaty and Brüel's analysis, ecological considerations have become a focus of public interest in a way that could not have been anticipated earlier, and this may greatly influence international law about the straits. If all three straits were dammed, the Baltic Sea would become a fresh water lake. Even the damming of one or two straits would have an influence on the regime of the Baltic Sea that would be of concern to all coastal states.[39] For this reason alone, if for no other, a damming of the Sound or the Little Belt could hardly be done without a new treaty with all the Baltic states, even though the interests of non-littoral states in passage into the Baltic could be well served by the Great Belt and the Kiel Canal.

Mare Clausum Balticum?

In consequence of the political rivalry between the United States and the Soviet Union in the twentieth century and in view of the geographic position of Russia, Soviet jurists have argued the Baltic Sea should be a "closed sea". The Soviet legal view suits its national strategic interests better than the consensus of the legal profession, which in recent centuries upheld the doctrine of Hugo Grotius, who argued for "freedom of the seas".[40] The Grotian concept fit the expanding world commerce and naval power of the Atlantic states, but the closed sea concept hibernated in the Russian Empire since the days of Peter the Great.[41] From time to time the Tsar took initiatives to keep the British out of the Baltic without much success, but the idea of freedom of the seas everywhere except in the regional seas of the Soviet Union, which is the doctrine postulated by Soviet jurists, essentially continues a Russian tradition.

The Soviet doctrine of the "closed sea" was first developed in two books published around 1950, one by Dranov on the Straits of the Black Sea and one by Molodtsov on the Baltic Straits. This was at the peak of the "Cold War", which influenced the language used in both the East and West.[42] Dranov and after him Molodtsov distinguish among three categories of straits: (1) those leading into internal seas, i.e., seas surrounded by one state, which should be within the exclusive jurisdiction of that state; (2) those leading into closed seas, i.e., seas surrounded by two or more states, the regime of which must be regulated by the coastal states that are most interested in the freedom of navigation and the security in that sea; and (3) those connecting high seas and oceans. In the interest of international trade, shipping by non-littoral states is permitted to and from the closed sea. After 1951 the writings of the two authors were incorporated into text books on international law in the Soviet Union.

A 1956 international law manual for the navy, edited by Bakhov, further developed the closed sea doctrine and distinguished three types: (1) those without natural connection to another sea (Caspian Sea); (2) those in which the straits were regulated by the regime of an international convention (Baltic Sea); and (3) those not regulated by an international convention (Sea of Okhotsk). All three types were also characterized by not having an internationally significant water route passing through them. The Soviet authors were referring to the Mediterranean and the North Sea, which they consider as falling into another category than the Black Sea and Baltic Sea. The Mediterranean and the North Sea in their view are parts of the world ocean.

In western literature "closed sea" is an antonym of "high (open) sea". To avoid confusion that may be caused by differences in usage the Soviet writer S.V. Malinin proposed the replacement of "closed sea" by "regional sea", defined by four legal requirements: (1) a particular geographic configuration of the coast; (2) surrounded by a limited number of states; (3) access to the sea through narrow approaches; and (4) absence of international maritime routes. According to this view of international law, the entry of the merchant vessels of non-littoral states could not be prohibited into a regional sea, but their warships could be denied. All the vessels of the littoral states would enjoy the right of free navigation outside the territorial waters in a regional sea.

This development of Soviet legal theory on the international law of the sea has been diametrically opposed to western thinking in these matters in the last three centuries. At the end of the Middle Ages several western claims to extension of sovereignty over parts of the open sea had been made, and other claims to closing parts of the sea to non-littoral states had been made in the seventeenth century by Denmark and Sweden in the Baltic. In the eighteenth century Russia, by agreements with the other littoral states, had tried to keep the British navy out of the Baltic. In the Treaty of Dorpat (1920) with Finland and Estonia, the young Soviet state had tried to continue this Russian tradition of neutralizing the Baltic and keeping British warships out. But western jurists and their governments argued for freedom of the seas from the seventeenth century onward, described by Cornelius Van Bynkershoek in *De Dominio Maris* (1702) by the distinction between a maritime belt, to be considered under the control of the littoral state, and the high seas, over which no sovereignty could be exercised.[43] By the late nineteenth century this legal view was almost universally recognized in national law and customary international law.

L. Oppenheim later described the open sea as the oceans, branches of the oceans known under special names, and branches of these branches of oceans, which are also known under their own names, e.g., the Baltic Sea and Gulf of Bothnia. To all these areas, he wrote, the principle of "freedom of the open sea" applies.[44] Typical of the modern view of "freedom of the high seas" are the rubrics of Starke: (a) the high seas can never be under the sovereignty of any one particular state; (b) absolute freedom of navigation on the high seas is allowed for vessels of all nations whether merchantmen or warships; (c) no state may exercise jurisdiction in a given sea over ships not bearing its flag; (d) a state may, as a general rule, exercise jurisdiction over a particular ship only in virtue of the maritime flag under which that ship sails; (e) every state and its citizens are entitled to make use of the high seas for laying submarine cables and oil pipelines, for the conduct of fisheries, and for scientific or technical purposes; (f) absolute freedom of flight above the sea exists for all aircraft.[45]

Negotiations for the 1958 Geneva Convention on the High Seas assumed that the Baltic Sea with the Gulf of Bothnia and the Gulf of Finland were parts of the high (open) seas, and that the Baltic Straits were international straits connecting two parts of the high seas. But the Soviet jurists have argued that historic treaties and conventions concerning the Baltic and its straits have made the Baltic a closed sea. The Sound Dues Convention of 1857 has been cited to support the claim that the Baltic Straits are under the "control" of international conventions concluded by Baltic powers. In addition, Molodtsov, writing in 1950, based his arguments on the history of Danish and Swedish claims to a closed sea in the Baltic, on the armed neutrality conventions of 1780 and 1800, on the secret Russo-German *mare clausum* agreement of 1907.[46] Thus, Soviet jurists have attempted to restructure international law by reinterpreting the past to conform to newly-devised concepts, theories, and philosophies designed specifically to restrict an even eliminate the possibility of foreign influences extending to areas of vital interest to the Soviet Union.[47]

Sweden, whose foreign trade over the centuries has been carried primarily in foreign vessels, considers the Baltic an "open sea". The Federal Republic of Germany for reasons of both shipping and security seeks a regime in which the littoral states of the Baltic would have no more rights, except for their territorial sea and economic zone, then non-littoral maritime states. Bonn would have preferred to delete Part IX of the 1980 Draft Convention (Informal Text) of the UN Law of the Sea Conference. Strictly followed, Article 122, which defines an "enclosed or semi-enclosed sea," could be applied to seas where the Soviet Union has important interests but is not littoral state: the Mediterranean Sea, the Persian (Arabian) Gulf, the South China Sea, the Caribbean Sea, the Gulf of Mexico.[48] The Soviet Union made some attempts to have the article changed, so that the Mediterranean Sea would be excluded from the definition. Essentially, Moscow and the Eastern bloc states would like the concept of an "enclosed sea" applied to the Baltic and Black seas. The states of the Eastern bloc prefer to carry their foreign trade in their own ships, but they favor freedom of the seas in cross-trading. They do not admit that freedom of navigation is restricted in any way in seas that connect other seas and oceans, such as the Mediterranean Sea, the North Sea, the Caribbean Sea, and the Sea of Japan,[49] but they want special rules for seas on which the Soviet Union is a coastal state, namely, the Baltic and Black seas.[50]

None of the Soviet writers has denied non-littoral merchant vessels free passage through the Baltic Straits or the international waters of a closed sea. The argument has been limited to naval ships, research vessels, and especially aircraft. The fishing boats of non-littoral states can no longer work in the Baltic Sea, except by permission of a coastal state, because the entire area has become either a territorial sea or an economic zone of one of the coastal states.

Chapter 5

PROSPECTS FOR PROSPERITY AND PEACE

Baltic Trade

The Baltic Sea is a busy sea, carrying a wealth of marine trade and ferry traffic. Its ports serve the major cities of seven countries with a foreign trade of imports and exports serving industrial, mining, and agricultural areas. Map 9 shows graphically and comparatively the amount of cargo handled by the many Baltic ports.

Ferry cargo is included in the port statistics of the Federal Republic of Germany but not in those of Denmark and Sweden. Rødby, Denmark, would otherwise have had the same large symbol as Puttgarden, Federal Republic of Germany, at the other end of the busy ferry route across the Fehmarn Belt. The symbols for Lübeck (Travemünde) and Kiel have also been inflated by ferry cargo.

Copenhagen, the old transit port for Baltic trade and competitor with Gothenburg for primacy among Nordic ports, is no longer the dominating center of seaborne transport on the Baltic Straits. The old Hanseatic city of Rostock has become a serious competitor. Until 1945 Rostock was in the traffic shadow of Hamburg and Stettin, since it had only a local hinterland, but it has been made the port of the German Democratic Republic and has some transit traffic with the other communist countries.

The largest ports in the Baltic Sea serve the densely populated southern and southeastern coasts of the region. Most of the important intra-Comecon trade, however, moves across the land borders south of the Baltic. Thus, the heavy traffic handled in the large Baltic ports does not adequately reflect the population distribution but rather indicates that Poland as well as the Soviet Union are large exporters of bulk commodities. Poland is the second largest coal exporter in the world (45 million tons a year).

Coal in recent years has accounted for three-fourths of Poland's seaborne exports and dominates both port areas of the country, the twin ports of Gdansk-Gdynia and the Oder estuary port of Szczecin (Stettin). The coal mines and the heavy industrial district are in the extreme south of Poland, about equidistant from the two port areas. Port-oriented shipyards and other heavy industries have in recent decades turned the Baltic ports into a manufacturing district that vies with Warsaw for second position among Poland's industrial regions.

The Soviet Union ranks high as exporter of both oil and coal. Its oil exports in recent years have been well over 100 million tons, with the main sea terminals on the Black Sea. Poland and the German Democratic Republic receive most of their oil by pipeline from the Soviet Union. Finland and to a lesser extent Sweden import Soviet oil across the Baltic Sea so that tanker traffic through the Baltic Straits is less heavy than might be expected. But this situation would change if the Soviet Union radically increased its oil exports to northwestern Europe or if the Soviet oil exports were drastically reduced, for this might force the German Democratic Republic and Poland as well as Finland to obtain more of their oil on the world market outside the Baltic area. In the longer perspective even the Soviet Union might become a net importer of oil.

The American Central Intelligence Agency in 1979 published a rather pessimistic projection on the expansion of the Soviet oil production, but that projection was based on expectations of technal difficulties in getting the oil economically out of the ground from the swamplands of western Siberia rather than on insufficient reserves. Technical expertise and equipment from the West, puchased by Moscow in an atmosphere of economic and military détente with Washington, could change these predictions. But substantially increased Soviet oil exports in the 1980s will probably require a rather rapid defrosting of relations between the superpowers. In 1981 the negotiation of a gas export agreement with Western Europe, providing a substitute for oil and moving by pipe south of the Baltic, seemed closer to realization.

In any case, since the Cuban missile crisis of 1962, the Soviet Union has moved vigorously to create a first-class navy as well as build a large merchant marine and a world-wide fishing fleet. Admiral Sergei Gorshkov, commander of the Soviet navy, had to argue his case for a powerful navy among the chiefs of staff, mostly army generals. He launched his expansion program as a "package deal" that would include the merchant marine and the fishing fleet. He recognized that, even in peacetime, fishing fleets and the merchant marine can add to intelligence-gathering services, although their economic justification ultimately lies in their proper fields of operation.

The Soviet fishing fleet was very successful in the 1960s and early 1970s. However, the proclamation of exclusive fisheries zones up to 200 miles from shore by a large number of coastal states will undoubtedly reduce some of the gains of the Soviet distant-water fleets. The Soviet merchant fleet of dry cargo vessels increased at a rate of 5.0 percent a year between 1969 and 1978 as against 3.4 percent for the world fleet.

The Soviet merchant marine can earn its way through cross-trading under a competent business management and even make a positive contribution to the

93

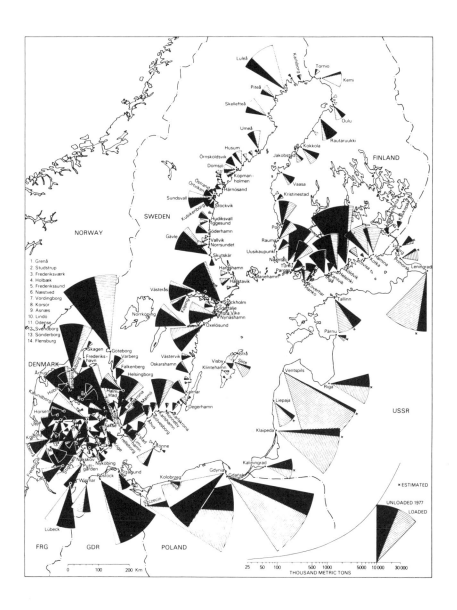

Map 9. Cargo Handled in Baltic Ports

Soviet balance of payments. Most of its costs are in non-convertible rubles and its cash flow in much desired hard currency. It has a comparative advantage of low labor costs but the disadvantage of being an outsider in the trade of the western democratic states. The Soviet Union is a compact land empire, indeed, the largest the world has ever known, but is is a second-rate trading nation, and most of its trade is with the other European communist countries, largely handled by land transport across their borders.

Leningrad, the second-largest metropolitan region in the Soviet Union after Moscow, is a large general cargo port, serving the leading machine-manufacturing center in the country. Among the new developments in transportation is a "land-bridge" for containers by way of the Transsiberian Railway to East Asia. Some containers from the West are first shipped by sea to Leningrad, others go directly by rail to Moscow, and then sent eastward. Riga, which is closer to Moscow than Leningrad, is rapidly becoming an alternative port for general cargo, including containers. With respect to the port statistics shown on Map 9 for the Soviet Union, no figures have been published and the symbols on the map are based on Western estimates.

In many leading Baltic ports, such as Szczecin, Gdynia, Gdańsk, Klaipeda, or Ventspils, shipments far exceed receipts, while in the ports that mainly serve metropolitan cities, such as Copenhagen, Stockholm, and Helsinki, imports prevail. Here also bulk cargo, primarily oil, accounts for the large tonnages. In Finland, the state-owned Neste Corporation dominates the oil trade, with two-thirds of all the oil imported from the Soviet Union going to oil refineries at Sköldvik and Naantali. These flows stay within the Baltic and come primarily from Klaipeda (Memel) in Lithuania and Ventspils in Latvia, which had a capacity of some 18 million tons, and a branch line from the large "Friendship Pipeline". Poland and the German Democratic Republic get much of their crude oil from the Soviet Union through pipelines to inland refineries, but increasing quantities also come from the Persian Gulf and elsewhere through the Great Belt to Baltic refineries at Rostock and Gdańsk. A new refinery at Gdańsk has been served by six 150,000-ton tankers that bring crude from the Persian Gulf and North Africa. They are the largest vessels that can pass the threshold at Darss. The oil products to Baltic Sweden and Finland arrive from three refineries on the Belts at Stigsnaes, Kalundborg, and Fredericia, and from several refineries in Gothenburg and points to the north in addition to the Oslofjord and the Norwegian west coast. Most oil companies now maintain a refinery on the Baltic approaches for the Nordic market, but some cargoes may still come from other refineries around the North Sea or the English Channel.

Oil has long dominated world shipping, and its transfer through international straits has naturally caused public concern about actual and potential damage to the marine and coastal environment. The Baltic Straits are similarly affected. Commodities other than oil, shipped in smaller quantities, primarily chemicals and explosives, are also potential threats to the environment. The pulp and paper industry, in which Sweden and Finland are major world producers, has been a heavy consumer of chemicals. Moreover, Swedish exports of explosives from the Karlskoga area have been shipped by small cargo vessels from Lake Vänern and the Göta Älv - through the center of Gothenburg - or by train to Varberg on the Kattegat. The amount of Soviet exports of explosives are not known, but they probably have been passing through the Baltic Straits.

A special problem has arisen between Denmark and Sweden in connection with the sea transport of nuclear waste from Swedish reactors to fuel recovery plants in Britain (Windscale) or France (La Hague). The container-carrying vessels have been moving through the Great Belt with the approval of the Danish authorities. But the Danes have objected to the transport of radioactive material through the Sound, so close to their capital city. The plant site at Barsebäck, just north of Malmö, poses special problems, but no decision by the two countries had been taken up to 1981. An alternative route for the Barsebäck containers would be by rail to the south coast of Skåne and from there by the T-Route. The new waste containers can withstand the pressure of a 2,500-meter water column, which is far beyond the depths encountered along the projected routes. Moreover, on these container vessels the Danes require pilots all the way to Skagen.

International Scientific Cooperation

The hydrological, geophysical, and biological characteristics of the Baltic Sea are of special interest to Denmark, Sweden, West and East Germany, Poland, Finland, and the Soviet Union. Although these states bridge different political ideologies, their concern about the optimal exploitation of marine resources and environmental pollution is somewhat similar and they all seek sound scientific information about the Baltic Sea. About 350 scientists have been working in 19 agencies or organizations that deal with marine science or resource problems either directly of indirectly.[1]

The International Council for the Exploration of the Sea (ICES), with headquarters at Charlottenlund, a suburb of Copenhagen, was founded in 1902, but its present constitution is based on a 1964 convention. The 18 members of the Council include all the European countries on the Atlantic Ocean and the Baltic Sea plus Canada and the United States. The main areas of its interest are the North Atlantic and the adjacent water bodies, such as the Kattegat and the Baltic Sea. Committees and working groups present recommendations on cooperative scientific work and on measures to aid the fisheries and to reduce pollution to the member governments of the Council. Research on the Baltic Sea is quite important in the work of ICES.

The Scientific Committee on Oceanic Research (SCOR) is a non-governmental, global organization with about 35 member countries, among them all the coastal states of the Baltic. SCOR holds general meetings every second year and has about a dozen working groups - mostly concerned with basic science and a few with environmental questions, such as the SCOR Working Group 42 on Pollution of the Baltic. The ICES/SCOR Working Group on the Study of Pollution of the Baltic was organized in Helsinki in 1971, with the secretariat provided by ICES in Copenhagen. Since 1973 seven tasks have been undertaken: (1) Study of the exchange of matter and water within the North Sea; (2) an open sea experiment; (3) development of an explanatory model of Baltic Sea circulation, followed by field observations; (4) a lateral boundary layer experiment; (5) the establishment of open sea multidisciplinary continuous monitoring stations; (6) biological productivity studies at fixed stations; and (7) a determination of toxic substances throughout the food chain. The Working Group consists of scientists from coastal states, who are drawn from both ICES and SCOR.

The International Hydrological Decade (IHD), organized by UNESCO in 1965-1974, led to a joint study by the Baltic states of the water balance of the Baltic Sea. In 1975 IHD became a permanent program (IHP), which has continued this cooperation through a group of experts on the water and material balance of the Baltic. They meet every second year and invite interested water scientists to attend.

The Nordic Council makes recommendations to the national parliaments and to the Nordic Council of Ministers. It initiated the Nordic Convention on the Environment, which was signed in 1974 and ratified in 1976, and it was one of the initiators of the Helsinki Convention of 1974 to reduce marine pollution.

The Helsinki Convention was initially implemented by the Interim Baltic Marine Environment Protection Commission known as the Helsinki Commission. Upon ratification of the convention in 1980 the Helsinki Commission (HELCOM) gained permanent status. It has a secretariat in Helsinki and two permanent working groups, the Scientific-Technological Working Group, dealing with water protection technology, setting criteria and standards, and monitoring the marine environment, and the Maritime Working Group, concerned with problems of pollution from vessels, primarily oil. Among the *ad hoc* groups set up by the permanent working groups is one by the maritime group to carry out joint field experiments of tagging oil residues from tankers. HELCOM also works through conferences, symposia, and special meetings arranged by the member states. It collaborates with other organizations such as ICES, IMCO, and the Baltic Marine Biologists organization. Special cooperative projects are carried out by member countries under the auspices of HELCOM, such as joint research in the Kattegat - Straits area by Denmark, Federal Republic of Germany, and Sweden.

The Nordic Council for Marine Biology was founded in 1956 to promote cooperation between the Nordic universities and their marine biological stations and is now funded by the Nordic Council of Ministers while the Nordic Council for Physical Oceanography, founded in 1966, is a parallel organization.

The Danish-Swedish Committee on Pollution of the Sound was formed in 1960. It had four working groups: on bacteriology, fishery biology, hydrography, and sanitary engineering. The results of their investigations were published. Then, the Convention on Protection of the Sound from Pollution was signed in 1974 and ratified in 1975. The Convention provided guidelines for the treatment of sewage and industrial wastes and for control measures to keep pollutants from exceeding recommended levels. It established a Sound Commission. Chairmanship of the commission alternates between the two coastal states; the secretariat moves with the chairman, while a working group does the practical work, convening experts when needed.

The Committee for the Gulf of Bothnia, formed in 1972, investigates long-term physical, chemical, and biological trends in cooperation with HELCOM, which is responsible for international research in adjacent waters. Swedish and Finnish government agencies signed the original documents, but the practical work is handled by a permanent working group which meets when appropriate.

Scientific and marine resource conservation agencies for the Baltic Sea have been established to include both the western states and the Soviet bloc. But the communist states and Finland have also created some agencies of their own.

The International Baltic Sea Fishery Commission (IBSFC), the administrative body of the Gdańsk Convention of 1973, had its headquarters in Warsaw with all the coastal states as members. Denmark and the Federal Republic of Germany are expected to be replaced by the European Community. Moreover, the Soviet Union, Poland, and the German Democratic Republic cooperate on fisheries questions and on the ecology of the coastal waters of the Baltic, with participation by Romania and Bulgaria to share their experience with the Black Sea. The three Baltic countries have formed a working group to prepare a monograph on the ecology of the Baltic.

Finland and the Soviet Union have collaborated in the Finnish-Soviet Working Group for the Protection of the Gulf of Finland, which was formed in 1976 and replaced another group that had been formed in 1969. The group meets every year and various symposia are arranged. Sub-groups deal with intercalibration of chemical methods and monitoring of the Gulf of Finland, the use of biological parameters, mathematical modelling, protection of the marine environment, oil pollution prevention, and fisheries problems. In addition, the Oder Haff Commission, formed by the German Democratic Republic and Poland, works on hydrographical, biological, and pollution projects in the lagoon-like mouth of the Oder river.

The Commission for Economic and Technological-Scientific Cooperation between Denmark and the Soviet Union has agreed to cooperate on, among other matters, the natural and human influence on the marine ecosystems of the Baltic, including the Belts and the Sound, while the Soviet-Swedish Committee on Economic, Scientific, and Technological Cooperation in 1971 decided to establish a mixed working group on environmental qualities to arrange symposia, compare measurements, organize joint marine expeditions, exchange of experts, and so forth.

Conferences of Baltic oceanographers have been held regularly every second year since 1957, hosted by the coastal states in rotation. Six hydrological conferences had already been held in the years before World War II. Physical and chemical problems of the Baltic Sea have been discussed, with more attention to pollution in recent years. The conferences are open to any interested persons and papers have been made public. Baltic Marine Biologists (BMB), founded in Rostock, German Democratic Republic in 1968, arranges symposia every second year in coastal states by rotation. They are open to all interested scientists and emphasize basic research and, in recent years, environmental problems. Some working groups have arranged joint investigations. The BMB cooperates with HELCOM, ICES and SCOR.

The recent introduction of exclusive economic zones by coastal states in the Baltic may increase the national interests in scientific investigations, but perhaps unnecessary rigidity and formalization will be avoided. Irrespective of political ideologies and economic systems, scientists in the coastal states agree that the Baltic ecosystem is in a delicate balance, which could easily be upset through the careless actions by man or stabilized and improved through cooperation among all parties concerned.

Measured by progress made by the time the Baltic Convention was ratified in 1980, there seems to be a gap between the three Nordic countries and the three countries of the Comecon, primarily due to the uneven standards of living. To comply with the convention, the contracting party must make heavy investments in treatment plants for industrial and municipal sewage, among other things. In times of economic crisis it may be difficult to find a place for these investments in the budgets of municipalities and manufacturing companies. To illustrate the point, in the summer of 1980 a mass swimming race with hundreds of participants was held in the center of metropolitan Stockholm, but long stretches of the most popular Polish beaches were closed to the public because of unsuitable water. Before the program of massive investments in municipal treatment plants was instituted in Sweden, the situation was similar at some Swedish towns on the Baltic. There will apparently be a time-lag before the countries of the Comecon catch up with the Nordic countries in the municipal and industrial investments necessary for compliance with the convention, but the high population pressure on the coasts of the Comecon countries may encourage such investments.

In sum, the degree of international cooperation for scientific research and the preservation of the marine environment in the Baltic Sea had been substantial, and with improved economic conditions the Comecon countries are likely to contribute more to this effort.

Military Force in the Baltic Region

The titanic naval battle off the west coast of northern Jutland from 31 May to 1 June 1916 between the British Grand Fleet and the German *Hochseeflotte* was the last major battle at sea in which aircraft had no part. The radically changed relations between sea and air power in the decades following the First World War indicated to the littoral states of the Baltic Sea that major navy vessels no longer had a place in their Baltic fleets. Strategists argued that naval vessels and airplanes should be garaged in rock tunnels when not at sea or in the air, and their views were confirmed by the Japanese attack on Pearl Harbor in December 1941.

The economics of military transportation dictate that a future conventional war between NATO and Warsaw Pact forces will be a land war to the south of the Baltic Sea. The reasons for this strategy were already evident in the First and Second World Wars, for while sea transport is cheaper, it is slower. In peacetime only bulk cargo is transported in coastal waters when there are inland road and rail alternatives, and in military operations speed is at a premium. Moreover, sea targets are easier preys to enemy air force and land-based missiles than land targets, and the average sea unit represents a much larger investment than the average land unit.

Since World War II the Soviet Union has maintained a vast superiority in troops and conventional weapons - artillery and tanks - for a land war in Western Europe, and they are positioned primarily in the German Democratic Republic. The North European plain, to the south of the Baltic Sea, has been the traditional marching area for troops heading east or west.

The Warsaw Pact has also maintained considerable superiority in the Baltic Sea with some 500 naval units against the 200 units of NATO. There are two reasons for stationing large marine units in the Baltic Sea: First, the belief that naval vessels will tie down enemy naval and air forces and prevent them from making a surprise attack, assuming that hiding places can be found where the vessels will be sufficiently protected. Second, the expectation that submarines carrying nuclear missiles can change position more easily than landbased launchers and that they will be more difficult to locate in the Baltic Sea with its halocline. However, military analysts have generally assumed that the major Soviet navy vessels will leave the Baltic before the outbreak of hostilities.

The Warsaw Pact maintains two regiments, a total of five to six thousand men, that can be lifted over the Baltic in hovercrafts and other landing crafts with little or no preparation. In addition, two divisions, some 20,000 men, can be shipped by commercial vessels. If such vessels were concentrated in advance, the lifting capacity could be increased considerably, and the availability of troops rather than vessels would set the limit, perhaps permitting the shipment of up to 15 divisions or about 150 thousand men.

Warsaw Pact forces have carried out at least three landing exercises in the Baltic from 1978 to 1980: (1) in June-July 1978 the Soviets made a landing at Taga Bay on Saaremaa Island, the southernmost of the two large islands off the west coast of Estonia, with enough ship capacity, including merchant vessels, for a regiment or three to four thousand soldiers, from the Kaliningrad area. The landing craft had strong protection from naval and air forces; (2) a similar landing was made in June 1980 in the southern part of Balticum where the transport distances were shorter, with somewhat less capacity of hovercraft and landing craft but with enough space for another regiment on the participating merchant vessels; (3) finally, exercise *Waffenbrüderschaft* in September 1980 was carried out with a hovercraft capacity of more than a regiment of Soviet, Polish, and German troops, and the landing was made on Rügen and Usedom off the coast of the German Democratic Republic.[2]

An East-West conflict in Europe with conventional weapons would probably be a land war, with operations in the Baltic a sideshow. However, a Warsaw Pact attempt to overrun the northern NATO flank with thrusts from Murmansk and through the Baltic approaches must be rated a high probability opening. It would emphasize the marine forces of the two blocs. A NATO attack through the Baltic is highly unlikely, given the present relations of the marine forces and the geopolitical situation of the Baltic region, but the build-up of the American Rapid Deployment Force, primarily designed for the Indian Ocean and the Persian Gulf area, could change these relations somewhat in a longer perspective.

The Rapid Deployment Force by 1985 may have the capacity to place 100,000 men with equipment anywhere "beyond the seas" three weeks after the command, especially if there were forced construction of supply ships that could be sent ahead to the crisis area. In 1981 at most a division of 16 to 20 thousand men could reach the crisis area within three weeks, even with the help of troop transport planes. But the Rapid Deployment Force would be of greater importance for the strategic situation in the Norwegian Sea and the

North Atlantic, including the North Sea, since both power blocs would hesitate to bring large marine units into the Baltic Sea.

In December 1979 NATO decided to place 572 nuclear missiles in Western Europe: 108 Pershing-2 ballistic missiles powered by rockets and 464 cruise missiles (Tomahawks) powered by jet engines. The Tomahawks fly at low altitude and thus are difficult to pick up by radar, but they have a speed of only 600-800 km/hour. The new medium-range weapons will be deliverd beginning in 1983, and in the meantime they provide leverage for negotiations with the Soviet Union about reduction in the nuclear balance in Europe.

According to the Institute of Strategic Studies in London the Soviets in the summer of 1980 already had 160 mobile SS-20s placed on their territory, most of them targeted on Western Europe. These modern weapons have a range of 4,800 km and carry three warheads with an explosive power of 150 kilotons of TNT each. They are replacing the SS-4s and SS-5s, which were first deployed in 1959 and which had a shorter range. The deployment rate for SS-20s has been increased from one per week to one per five days. Meanwhile, the Soviet Union is also producing short-range or "battlefield" nuclear missiles. All these new weapons on both sides of the superpower armaments lie in the "gray area" between the strategic and the tactical.

Most of the new NATO-missiles, all the Pershings and 112 cruise missiles, are planned for deployment in the Federal Republic of Germany. The United Kingdom is expected to have 112 cruise missiles, Italy 96, and the Netherlands and Belgium each 48. It should be noted that SALT-2 allows the United States to keep 3,500 cruise missiles at American bases. By 1982 the B-52s may be in a position to carry 20 missiles per plane and drop them, say, over the Norwegian Sea, out of reach of the Soviet air defense. This would be a greater threat to the Soviet Union than the relatively few Europe-based missiles.

The new nuclear weapon system of NATO and the Warsaw Pact may change the strategic situation in the Baltic area since some potential trajectories pass over the Baltic Sea and over neutral Sweden and Finland. The Soviet Union may find it attractive in a "gray period" to secure the neutral territories, especially Sweden, for a forward anti-missile defense, although land-based Anti-Ballistic Missile systems (ABM) are lacking since the superpowers in SALT-1 agreed to limit the construction of the exceedingly expensive ABMs, and the only Soviet ABM, around Moscow, has a range of some 300 km. The cruise missiles, moreover, are non-interceptable by any known ABM system, for they fly too low and follow unpredictable paths between the launching areas and the predictable targets.

For obvious geographic reasons, the probability for an aggressive policy by NATO against the neutrals, Sweden and Finland, must be considered very low or nil. The risk of a preemptive occupation of part of Sweden in a crisis by either power bloc may seem theoretically greater in 1982 because the Soviet

Union has reached nuclear parity with the United States. The two most sensitive areas would be southern Sweden, adjacent to the Baltic approaches, and the North Calotte, between northernmost Norway and the Kola Peninsula. Any action by NATO against Sweden, however, would be based on a risky calculation that the Soviet bloc would not respond out of fear of escalation. Finland is too close to the economic core of the Soviet Union for trespassing, and the 1948 treaty would immediately justify Soviet military support to Finland against any foreign intervention.

Neutral Sweden has maintained a rather strong military posture in the postwar period, a prerequisite for the Nordic balance. It has been one of the few countries in the world producing tanks, artillery, airplanes, and submarines. The burden of extensive armament production in a country of some eight million people can be eased only through large-scale production and substantial exports. But this option has been somewhat limited in a neutral country that has imposed on itself various restrictions prohibiting the sale of weapons to countries in politically unstable areas.

In Sweden, moreover, security discussions have followed two lines of argument: first, that defense should be based on the probability of an attack on Sweden. Since all experts agree that the probability is low, this argument has been favored by politicians who want to reallocate funds from the military to other sectors of the state budget. The second argument is that defense should be based on experience showing that many wars in the past have been unexpected low-probability conflicts. Since it takes a long time to build a proper defense against invasion attempts, the right level of Swedish forces would be one that offered a fair chance of turning back the strongest invasion forces now existing in the Baltic, that is, the Warsaw Pact forces.

In reviewing the prospects for peaceful collaboration in the Baltic region, it should be noted that the Federal Republic of Germany in 1980 exceeded Finland as the most important trading partner of the Soviet Union in the West. Fear of the Germans seems more a matter of the postwar past in Soviet foreign policy rather than the future, for Moscow has not only maintained good relations with the German Democratic Republic, its leading trading partner, but also with the Federal Republic of Germany. Germany over the centuries has had strong commercial ties not only with Russia but with all of eastern European states, more so than with Atlantic Europe, especially in the 1920s and 1930s.

Being a pillar of the European Community and with strong economic, political, and military links with the United States, the Federal Republic of Germany should be in a position to serve as a bridge between the two superpowers with their different philosophical and geopolitical backgrounds. Germany and the Soviet Union can cooperate from a position of strength and involvement, and these two Baltic powers also have the keys to a global disarmament process that could benefit the whole of mankind.

The costs of the arms race are obvious. The United States has been spending about five percent of its gross national product on arms, and its European allies have been devoting three to four percent to arms, which they can ill afford in addition to the escalating costs for their oil imports. Thus, Denmark and Belgium in 1980 found it politically difficult to honor the three percent annual increase (in real terms) in military spending that had been agreed to by the NATO members. The situation was even worse in the Soviet Union, which was estimated to have devoted 11-13 percent of its gross national product to the military budget, which apparently grew at a three percent annual rate. Very strong reasons on both sides of the Iron Curtain thus speak in favor of reopened negotiations, with cooperation in the Baltic region especially important to mutual trust.

The narrow waters of the Baltic separate the market economy of the West from the centrally planned economy to the East. They also separate the Warsaw Pact from NATO, but here the buffer zone is wider, including two neutral countries, Finland and Sweden, who have found it in their interest to stay outside the military alliances, contributing to the political stability in Northern Europe.

The Cold War of the 1950s over such issues of direct concern to the Baltic region as the division of Germany and the status of Berlin have been followed by improved East-West relations, culminating in the policy of détente of 1972 and the Helsinki Accords of 1975. No country in the Baltic area has claims to the territory of any other country. The eventual reunification of the two parts of Germany seems to be no longer a cause of conflict but rather a matter for cooperation between the two German states in agreement with their allies.

The United States and the Soviet Union cooperated in many fields in the 1970s and their respective European allies have been eager to share in the advantages of cooperating with the superpower of the opposite side as well as with the smaller powers of that camp. East-West trade and both economic and cultural agreements have multiplied. Large credits for modernization have been extended by countries and banks in the West to the communist countries of the East, especially to Poland, with the Federal Republic of Germany playing a central role in this development. The *Ostpolitik* has been a central political theme in the Federal Republic of Germany, while the Soviet Union perceived its new relations with West Germany as a basis for stability in western Europe. Finally, the regions of direct superpower confrontation in the 1970s were far away from the Baltic Sea.

With full awareness that the alternative is nuclear holocaust, the two superpowers could turn the Baltic region - characterized by postwar stability -into a testing ground for economic and social cooperation with long-term conflict management. The ideologies of Moscow and Washington, with their respective adherents, will be in conflict for a long time to come. But Finland,

Sweden, Denmark, and the Federal Republic of Germany have shown that they can successfully cooperate with the other littoral states of the Baltic: the Soviet Union, Poland and the German Democratic Republic. The burden lies upon Moscow and Washington to keep the Baltic Sea as a sea of peace in which trade may flourish, resources may be exploited equitably, and a healthy marine environment may be preserved. In that way the Baltic Straits may continue to serve the commerce of all nations and the security of Europe.

DOCUMENTARY APPENDICES

I. Ordinance of 27 February 1976 Covering the admission of foreign warships and military aircraft to Danish territory in time of peace.

II. Proclamation of 3 June 1966 (No. 366) concerning the admission to Swedish territory of foreign naval vessels and military aircraft.

III. Recommendations on navigation through the entrances to the Baltic Seas by IMCO, November 1975.

I.   Ordinance of 27 February 1976 covering the admission of foreign
      warships and military aircraft to Danish territory in time of peace.[1]

Part 1. General Provisions

1. (1) This Ordinance shall apply to the admission of foreign warships
and military aircraft to Danish territory when Denmark as well as the
State by which the vessel or aircraft is owned are in a state of peace.

(2) Other vessels and aircraft which are owned or used by a foreign
state and which are not employed exclusively for commercial purposes
shall be equated with foreign warships and military aircraft in the application of the provisions of this Ordinance.

(3) For the purpose of this Ordinance the term "passage" means
innocent passage within the meaning of international law.

(4) Where advance permission is required pursuant to this Ordinance, the application for such permission shall be submitted not less
than eight days in advance. Where advance notification of passage is required, such notification shall be given not less than three days in
advance of the proposed passage.

(5) The Minister of Defence may make exceptions to the provisions
of this Ordinance.

2. (1) For the purpose of this Ordinance the term "Danish territory"
means Danish land territory and Danish territorial waters and the air
space over these territories.
(2) Danish territorial waters embrace the territorial sea and internal
waters as defined in the relevant provisions in force at any given time.

Part 2. Warships

3. (1) Foreign warships shall enjoy the right of passage through the territorial sea subject to advance notification being given through diplomatic

1. English text provided by the Ministry of Foreign Affairs of Denmark in a note verbale of
11 October 1977. UN Doc. ST/LEG/SER. B/19, 13 June 1978, S. 150-152

channels, cf, however, subsection (4) below. For the vessels referred to in section 1, subsection (2), notification of passage shall not, however, be required.

(2) Where navigation within the territorial sea takes place in connection with passage of the Great Belt, Samsøe Belt or the Sound, notification shall not be required, cf., however, subsection (4) below.

(3) Foreign warships shall not be allowed during passage to stop or anchor in the territorial sea except where advance permission to do so has been obtained through diplomatic channels or where stopping or anchoring are incidental navigation or are rendered necessary by *force majeure* or by distress.

(4) For simultaneous passage of the territorial sea of more than three warships of the same nationality advance permission, obtained through diplomatic channels, is required. Passage of the Great Belt, Samsøe Belt or the Sound shall be allowed, however, subject to advance notification through diplomatic channels. Permission or notification, as the case may be, shall not be required for the vessels referred to in section 1, subsection (2).

4. (1) Warships may pass through or stay in internal waters where advance permission for such passage or stay has been obtained through diplomatic channels.

(2) Passage of Hollaenderdybet/Drogden and passage of the Little Belt and, in connection therewith, the necessary navigation by the shortest route through internal waters between Fyn, Endelave and Samsøe shall be allowed, however, subject to advance notification through diplomatic channels.

5. The permissions and notifications referred to in sections 3 and 4 shall not be required for vessels in distress. In the event of distress the vessel shall give international distress signal and notify Danish naval authority - possibly through a Danish coastal radio station.

6. (1) Warships may not without special permission conduct scientific or military activity within Danish territorial waters.

(2) Submarines are required to navigate on the surface while within Danish territorial waters.

(3) Warship shall show their naval or national flag while within Danish territorial waters. In port flags may, however, be used under traditional regulations governing the display of flags.

Part 3. Military Aircraft

7. (1) For flights over or landing in Danish territory of military aircraft advance permission, obtained through diplomatic channels, is required. This provision shall not apply to aircraft in distress and aircraft which, with the approval of Danish authorities, are conducting flights for humanitarian purposes.

(2) Permission to overfly or land in Danish territory will be granted only if an ordinary ICAO (International Civil Aviation Organization) flight schedule is submitted prior to the flight to the competent Danish air traffic service organ and if the flight is otherwise carried out in accordance with the guidelines set out by ICAO and the provisions relative to these guidelines laid down by Danish aeronautical authorities.

8. (1) Military aircraft may not without special permission conduct scientific or military activity within Danish territory.

(2) Military aircraft may carry permanent installation of weapons without ammunition and cameras without films or plates. Electronic equipment other than such as is required for navigation of the aircraft may not be used by military aircraft over Danish territory.

Part 4. Repeal

9. Royal Ordinance No. 356 of June 25, 1951,[2] governing the Admittance of Foreign Men-of-War and Service Aircraft to Danish Territory in Time of Peace is hereby repealed.

---

2. Reproduced in UN Doc. ST/LEG/SER.B/, p.369

I. **Proclamation of 3 June 1966 (no. 366) concerning the admission to Swedish territory of foreign naval vessels and military aircraft.**[1]

Article 1. For the purpose of this Proclamation Swedish territory shall mean the land territories and territorial waters as well as the air space above.

Article 2. The provisions of the Proclamation concerning naval vessels shall also apply to other vessels and hovercraft owned or used by a Foreign Power and employed for a non-commercial purpose. The provisions concerning military aircraft shall equally apply to other aircraft for a non-commercial purpose.

Article 3. If Sweden should be at war the Proclamation shall be void.

Articles 15 - 29 shall enter into force when the King in Council so ordains. When these Articles are in force, Articles 4, 5, and 7 - 14 shall not apply to naval vessels and military aircraft of belligerent Power.

General Provisions Applying to Naval Vessels and Military Aircraft of a Foreign Power.

Article 4. A naval vessel of a Foreign Power shall be admitted to through the territorial sea after notification through diplomatic channels. No such notification however, is, required for a passage through the territorial sea in the Oresund (the Sound) between the lines Kullen-Gilbjerghoven and Falsterbo Udde (Falsterbo Point)-the Stevn Lighthouse.

Admittance to Swedish territory for naval vessels in a case other than that referred to in the first paragraph requires permission. No permission, however, is required for a naval vessel in distress or when used by the Head of State of a Foreign Power when visiting Sweden.

Article 5. A military aircraft of a Foreign Power shall be admitted to pass through the air space above the territorial sea in the Oresund (the Sound) between the lines Kullen-Gilbjerghoved and Falsterbo Udde (Falsterbo Point) - the Stevn Lighthouse.

1. Unofficial Translation, Stockholm, 15 December 1968.

110

Admittance to Swedish territory of aircraft in a case other than that referred to in the first paragraph requires permission. No permission is, however, required for an aircraft in distress or when used by the Head of State of a Foreign Power when visiting Sweden.

Article 6. For naval vessels and military aircraft of a Foreign Power the Swedish regulations, where relevant, in respect of health pilotage, customs, traffic, port, airport and public order as well as the regulations regarding the use of a wireless station shall apply within Swedish territory. Instructions given by a Swedish Authority shall be followed.

Article 7. A naval vessel of a Foreign Power shall not stop or anchor or otherwise interrupt its voyage within Swedish territory without permission unless this is necessary for the safety of the vessel. Should a naval vessel have to interrupt its voyage or should it because of distress, enter internal waters, the vessel shall, if possible, make an international signal and notify a Swedish Authority of the circumstances.

Article 8. A naval vessel of a Foreign Power shall have its national flag hoisted when proceeding through the territorial waters. Submarines must keep to the surface. In internal waters a naval vessel shall proceed in pilotage waters, utilizing the services of a competent Swedish pilot.

Article 9. Military aircraft of a Foreign Power shall within Swedish territory be navigated within controlled air space and in accordance with the regulations applying to Civil Air Navigation unless in a special case the King in Council decides otherwise. Should an aircraft enter the territory because of distress, it shall, if possible, make an international signal and notify a Swedish Authority of the circumstances.

Article 10. Maps shall not be drawn or measuring carried out or sounding taken from a naval vessel or a military aircraft of a Foreign Power unless this is necessary for the safety of the vessel or the aircraft. Air photography is forbidden.

Article 11. A naval vessel or a military aircraft of a Foreign Power shall not without permission hold artillery exercises or such exercises as cannot in their entirety be carried out on board the vessel or the aircraft itself. Nor shall any maneuvring connected with warlike exercises take place.

Article 12. On board a military aircraft of a Foreign Power guns or cameras, other than those which are mounted on board the aircraft, as well as ammunition, explosives, photographic slides or films shall not be carried without special permission.

Article 13. Personnel of a naval vessel or a military aircraft of a Foreign Power shall not be disembarked at any place other than that for which visiting permission has been granted. Disembarked personnel shall not be regarded as having entered the realm. Disembarked personnel shall not carry arms without permission. An officer or a warrant officer may nevertheless carry a blank weapon forming part of the uniform. Armed troop shall not be carried on board an aircraft except by permission.

Article 14. The King in Council grants permission referred to in Articles, 4, 5, 7 and 11-13. The National Civil Aviation Administration, after consultation with the Supreme Commander of the Swedish Forces, may admit a military aircraft of a Foreign Power to enter Swedish territory, if the aircraft is unarmed and is used for transportation on behalf of the United Nations or for such transportation as corresponds to civil aviation transportation. Permissions which are granted by the King in Council shall be obtained through diplomatic channels.

Special Provisions Applying to Naval Vessels and Military Aircraft of a Belligerent Power.

Article 15. Naval vessels and military aircraft of a belligerent Power shall respect the Swedish neutrality. No act of war - including the arrest, capture or searching of a vessel or an aircraft - shall be undertaken within Swedish territory nor shall it be undertaken against any object or person within that territory. Swedish territory shall not be used as a base for war operations. Intelligence activities or operational control must not be carried out.

Article 16. A naval vessel of a belligerent Power shall be admitted to pass through the territorial sea for a maximum period of 24 consecutive hours. A submarine or a hovercraft, however, is only admitted to pass through the territorial sea in the Oresund (the Sound) between the lines Kullen-Gilbjerghoved and Falsterbo Udde (Falsterbo Point) - the Stevn Lighthouse. A naval vessel which has left the territorial sea may not return until at least 48 hours have elapsed.

Admission to Swedish territory in any other case than that referred to in the first paragraph is permitted only for a naval vessel in severe distress at sea and for a military hospital vessel or for such naval vessels as are fitted out and used exclusively for humanitarian purposes pursuant to a decision by the Commander-in-Chief of Military Area after consultation with the Commissioner of Civil (Defense) Area.

Article 17. Not more than three naval vessels of the same belligerent Power, or of allied belligerent Powers may be within Swedish territory at the same time.

Article 18. A military aircraft of a belligerent Power may, without undue deviations from its course enter the air space above the territorial sea in the Oresund (the Sound) between the lines Kullen-Gilbjerhoved and Falsterbo Udde (Falsterbo Point) - the Stevn Lighthouse.

Admission to Swedish territory in any case other than that referred to in the first paragraph is permitted only for an aircraft in distress or for an ambulance aircraft pursuant to a decision by the Supreme Commander of the Swedish Armed Forces.

Article 19. A naval vessel of a belligerent Power which is within Swedish territory when Articles 15 - 19 enter into force shall leave the territory within 24 hours. Should naval vessels of different belligerent Powers be in the same port, or at the same anchorage, and should these Powers not be allied, a period of at least 24 hours shall elapse between their respective times of departure. The naval vessels shall depart in the order in which they have arrived unless special circumstances give rise to some other arrangement. If a merchant vessel of a belligerent Power leaves a port or anchorage where there is also a naval vessel of an enemy Power, the naval vessel may leave 24 hours at the earliest after the merchant vessel had departed.

Article 20. A naval vessel of a belligerent Power shall not stop or anchor or otherwise interrupt its voyage within Swedish territory unless this is necessary for the safety of the vessel. Should a naval vessel have to interrupt its voyage or should it enter a prohibited area of the territory because of distress at sea, or should it not be able to leave the territory within the prescribed time limit, the vessel shall, if possible, make an international signal and notify a Swedish Authority of the circumstances.

Should a naval vessel enter a prohibited area of the territory because of severe distress at sea or should the vessel not be able to leave the territory within the prescribed time limit, the Commander-in-Chief of Military Area shall determine a reasonable respite within which the vessel shall leave the territory. It shall also rest with the Commander-in-Chief of Military Area to decide to what extent repairs may be carried out. In this respect it must be observed that no respite shall be allowed if it is obvious that the vessel cannot be made seaworthy within a reasonable period of time, that damage ensuing from an act of war must not be repaired, and that other repairs may be executed only to the extent which is necessary for the seaworthiness of the vessel. Should the limit of the respite which has been fixed be exceeded, the vessel shall be retained through the offices of the Commander-in-Chief of Military Area.

Article 21. A naval vessel of a belligerent Power shall always have its national flag hoisted when within Swedish Territory. Submarines must keep to the surface. In internal waters a naval vessel shall proceed only in pilotage waters, utilizing the services of a competent Swedish pilot. In the territorial sea the services of a pilot may be utilized only in severe distress at sea.

Article 22. A naval vessel of a belligerent Power may replenish its supplies pursuant to a decision by the Commander-in-Chief of Military Area if, when Articles 15 - 29 enter into force, the vessel is in internal waters, or in the event of a respite having been granted the vessel by virtue of Article 20. In this connection it should be observed that replenishing shall take place only to the extent needed to enable the vessel to reach the nearest port within its own territory.

Replenishing of supplies in any case other than that referred to in the first paragraph is permitted, pursuant to a decision by the Commander-in-Chief of Military Area after consultation with the Commissioner of Civil (Defense) Area for a military hospital vessel or of such naval vessels as are fitted out and used exclusively for humanitarian purposes, as well as for ambulance aircraft.

Article 23. A military aircraft of a belligerent Power which, because of distress, enters Swedish territory shall, if possible, make an international signal. Should a military aircraft have landed or alighted on water within the territory, the aircraft shall be retained through the offices of the Commander-in-Chief of Military Area. An ambulance aircraft, however, shall not be retained.

Article 24. Maps shall not be drawn on measuring carried out or sounding taken from a naval vessel or a military aircraft of a belligerent Power unless this is necessery for the safety of the vessel or the aircraft. Air photography is forbidden. Naval vessels or military aircraft shall not carry out exercises.

Article 25. A wireless installation on board a naval vessel or military aircraft of a belligerent Power shall not be used transmission of wireless communications in cases other than those of distress or for communication with a Swedish Authority via a Swedish radio station.

Article 26. Personnel of a naval vessel or a military aircraft of a belligerent Power shall not be disembarked unless the Commander-in-Chief of Military Area decides otherwise. Disembarked personnel shall not be regarded as having entered the realm

Special provisions applying to a ship which has been captured, etc.

Article 27. A foreign vessel which has been captured by a belligerent Power shall be admitted to pass through the territorial sea in the Oresund (the Sound) between the lines Kullen-Gilbjerghoved and Falsterbo Udde (Falsterbo Point)-the Stevn Lighthouse.

Admission to Swedish territory in any case other than that referred to in the first paragraph is permitted only for a captured vessel which is in severe distress at sea.

The provisions of Articles 6, 15, 20, 21, and 24 - 26 shall apply to a captured vessel which is within the territory. A captured vessel shall not be allowed to replenish its supplies within the territory.

Article 28. A Swedish ship, captured by a belligerent Power, and which enters Swedish territory shall not leave the territory without permission by the King in Council.

Article 29. The provisions of Article 27 shall, in applicable parts, govern the transportation of prisoners of war.

Application of Provisions

Article 30. Detailed provisions and instructions as to the application of this Proclamation are issued by the King in Council or, after authorization by the King in Council, by the Supreme Commander of the Swedish Armed Forces. In addition to the provisions of the Proclamation, such special regulations relative to admittance to Swedish territory apply as the King in Council may determine.

This Proclamation enters into force on July 1, 1966, whereafter the following proclamations shall become void...

III. Recommendation on navigation through the entrances to the Baltic Sea by IMCO, Noverber 1975

The Assembly

BEING AWARE of the close relationship between safety of navigation and the prevention of pollution from ships,

BEING ALSO AWARE of the urgent need to protect the vulnerable Baltic Sea Area which has been designated a special area against pollution.

NOTING that the navigation of large ships through the entrances to the Baltic Sea Area constitutes, due to the risk of grounding or collision, a potential danger of pollution of the entrances and due to the strong sea-current also pollution of the entrances and due to the strong sea-current also pollution of the entire Baltic Area,

NOTING ALSO that this passage at several places will be difficult to navigate,

TAKING NOTE of

- Resolution 5 - Intentional Pollution of the Sea and Accidental Spillages adopted by the International Conference on Marine Pollution, London 1973,
- Resolution A.159 (ES.IV) - Recommendation on Pilotage and
- Resolution A.156 (ES.IV) - Recommendation on the Carriage of Electronic Position-Fixing Equipment,

RECOMMENDS the following:

(a) that ships over 40,000 tons deadweight when passing through the entrences to the Baltic Sea, in view of the fact that 17 meters is the maximum obtainable depth without dredging in the area North East of Gedser and that the charted depths, even under normal conditions, may be decreased by as much as 2 meters due to unknown and moving obstructions, should:

   (ı) not pass the area unless they have a draught with which it is safe to navigate through it taking into account the possibility of depths being as much as 2 meters less than charted as mentioned above, additionally taking into account the possible changes in the indicated depth of water due to meteorological or other effects,

(II) participate in the radio position reporting system operating by the Government of Denmark,

(III) in certain areas in Store-Baelt (Hatterrev, Vengeancegrund and in the narrow route East of Langeland) when constrained by their draught show the signal prescribed in Rule 28 in the International Regulations for Presenting Collisions at Sea, 1972,

(b) that ships with a draught of 13 meters or more should furthermore:

(I) be equipped with a VHF radiotelephone installation, fitted with appropriate frequencies,

(II) have on board suitable electronic fixing equipment to make use of hyperbolic systems which will provide sufficient fixing accuracy for navigating in this area,

(III) use for the passage the pilotage services locally established by the coastal States,

(IV) be aware that anchoring may be necessary owing to the weather and sea conditions in relation to the size and draught of the ship and to the sea level and in this respect take special account of the information available from the pilot and from radio navigation information services in the area.

(c) that a routeing system be established so that ships referred to and complying with the recommendations contained in paragraphs (a) and (b) above can safely navigate into the Baltic.

NOTES TO CHAPTERS 1-5

Chapter 1

1. "Enclosed sea"is a descriptive term here, not be confused with the legal concept "enclosed or semi-enclosed sea" used in the Draft Convention (Informal Text) of the Third UN Conference on the Law of the Sea (UNCLOS III).

2. British geography books and atlases traditionally show a land hemisphere, with London and the Channel at its center, and a sea hemisphere, centered in the sea east of southern New Zealand, pointing up the favorable position of northwestern Europe and the North Atlantic sea route.

3. For passengers from the Baltic region an alternative to the ship passage through the Danish straits had existed before the modern period. A passage from Stockholm to New York probably went by ship to Lübeck, overland to Hamburg, by ship to the British east coast or directly to New York. In the former case, the Atlantic passage was made out of Liverpool after an overland journey in Britain. Attempts at avoiding the long detour around the Skaw is nothing new in the history of Baltic shipping. They were made by the Vikings who crossed the isthmus of the Jutland Peninsula at present Schleswig.

Chapter 2

1. H.U. Sverdrup, M.W. Johnson, and R.H. Fleming, *The Oceans: Their Physics, Chemistry and General Biology* (New York: Prentice Hall, 1942), pp. 11 ff.

2. The "Baltic Sea Area" includes the Kattegat. The border between the approach to the Baltic and the Skagerack, the approach to the North Sea proper, is drawn by the lattitude through Skagen (the Skaw), 57°N 44′8. Alternatively, the limit is drawn to a point somewhat further north on the Swedish side, Pater Noster at Marstrand.

3. Lewis M. Alexander, "The Seventh Session of the Third United Nations Conference on the Law of the Sea", *Geographical Review,* Vol. 69 (July 1979), p. 349.

4. This includes the history of navigation. More navigational skills have always been required from captains operating in the North Sea than from those moving between Baltic ports only. A ship loosing its bearings in the Baltic would come to a shore rather soon, but one in the North Sea could easily be blown into the North Atlantic and be lost if the captain could not measure his latitude and longitude.

5. See A. Thunberg, "Sjömätning och dess bakgrund", *Ymer*, Vol. 87 (1967), pp. 56 ff. Among ports that can receive large vessels are Gdańsk -Gdynia in Poland, Oxelösund, Nynäshamn and Luleå in Sweden and Sköldvik in Finland.

6. The continental shelf can extend beyond the 200-meter isobath where the superjacent water permits of exploitation of its resources according to the 1958 Geneva Convention on the Continental Shelf.

7. Nils-Axel Mörner, "Submarin Kvartärgeologi i Östersjön; några preliminära resultat och framtidsaspekter", *Ymer*, Vol. 93 (1973), p. 96.

8. UN Doc. A/CONF 62/C 2/L 11, 17 July 1974, Art 1, 2 (f).

9. Ivar Hessland, "Geologisk undersökning av Östersjöns botten," *Ymer*, Vol. 93 (1973), p. 42.

10. Z. Mikulski, "Inflow of River Water to the Baltic Sea in the Period 1951-1960", *Nordic Hydrology*, 1970:4, pp. 216-227.

11. Björn Ganning, "Östersjön - ett hydrografiskt och biologiskt problem", *Ymer*, Vol. 93 (1973).

12. *Finsk Sjöfart 1979* (with English summary), Helsinki, 1979. For a general discussion of winters in the Baltic, see W.R. Mead & Helmer Smeds, *Winter in Finland* (London, 1967).

13. Named for President Urho Kekkonen and for the national characteristic "Sisu" of trying hard and never giving up, ascribed to the Finns by their neighbors. The Swedish *Ymer* is a sister ship. She was used for an international research trip into the Arctic Ocean in 1980 in centennial memory of A.E. Nordenskiöld's northeast passage with the *Vega*. Only the Soviet Union, Finland, and Sweden can provide icebreakers for this type of trips - an indication of the countries in the world that have the most serious ice problems.

14. Bengt-Owe Jansson, "The Baltic - an Ecological Survey", *Industrial Pollution in the Baltic Environment*, The Federation of Swedish Industries, 1975.

15. L.E. Mattson, "Åtgärder mot vattenförorening från fartyg inom Östersjöområdet," *Svensk hamntidning*, Oct. 1976, pp. 217-228.

16. Finland-USSR (20 May 1965 and 5 May 1967); FRG-Denmark (9 June 1965); Denmark-Norway (8 December 1965 and 24 April 1968); Norway-Sweden (24 July 1968); Poland-DDR (29 September 1968); USSR-Poland (29 August 1969); Finland-Sweden (29 September 1972); DDR-Sweden (22 June 1976).

17. In addition to USSR-Sweden and the Poland-Denmark agreements, those between FRG-DDR, Denmark-DDR, Denmark-Sweden, and Sweden-Poland remain to be signed.

18. Paul Lydolph, *Geography of the USSR,* 3rd ed., (New York: Wiley, 1977), p. 175.

19. Doxiadis has listed this coastal preference among his general principles for future population distribution. C.A. Doxiadis, "The Coming World-City: Ecumenopolis," in Arnold Toynbee, *Cities of Destiny* (New York: McGraw-Hill, 1967). See also G. Alexandersson & T. Falk, "Changes in the Urban Pattern of Sweden 1960-1970: The Beginning of a Return to Small Urban Places?" *Geoforum*, 1974:18, pp. 87-92, and T. Falk, "Urban Turnaround in Sweden: The Acceleration of Population Dispersal 1970-1975," *Geojournal*, 1978: 2.1, pp. 27-34.

Chapter 3

1. The terminology is the same in German and Danish. The West Sea in those two languages is the North Sea.

2. Sten Carlsson, *Svensk historia II* (Stockholm: Bonniers, 1961).
   More details in A. Cullberg, *La politique du Roi Oscar I pendant la guerre du Crimée,* (Stockholm, 1912-1926) and Sven Eriksson, *Svensk diplomati och tidningspress under Krimkriget* (Stockholm, 1939)

3. Professor Ilmari Hustich of Helsinki, one of few Nordic authors who covers both economic and political geography in his writings, uses a simple triangle connecting the three largest metropolitan areas to indicate the economic core area of a country. For Finland and Sweden this method gives a good approximation to reality based on detailed data. The Swedish triangle has its corners in Stockholm, Gothenburg, and Malmö and thus one side on the West Coast. In the beginning of the last century, one corner would have been at Karlskrona, instead of at Malmö, and one side along the Baltic coast. In 1800, Karlskrona had 10,200 inhabitants and Malmö only 4,000. In 1970 Karlskrona had 63,300 inhabitants while Malmö had reached 277,300. See also T. Falk, *Urban Sweden*(Stockholm: EF1, 1976).

4. The increase in East-West Trade is probably a very small factor in this development. The most important explanation is presumably the high standard of living in western industrialized nations (high income, family car) which gives more individuals freedom of residence. Increasingly, employers locate their plants where people want to live. Plants go looking for people whereas a few decades ago people went looking for jobs. See Alexandersson & Falk, op cit. The Swedish population redistribution in the latest years agrees with the coastal preference in the choice of residence hypothesized by C.A. Doxiadis (1967).

5. The Swedish-speaking population of Finland now makes up a smaller group than the Finland-born residents of Sweden, which was about 300,000 in 1977.

6. The Finns were, and still are, in a worse position than their linguistic relatives in Hungary for whom German, French, Italian, and, more recently, English are the natural foreign languages. Neither Russian nor Swedish is spoken much outside their national territory. German, taught in high school, and, later, English have helped break the linguistic isolation of the Finns. After the Second World War, Swedish has provided the Finns with a *lingua franca* in the intensified Nordic cooperation.

7. L.A. Puntila, *Finlands politiska historia 1809-1966* (Helsingfors: Schildt, 1966), p. 73. This section leans heavily on Professor Puntila's lucid treatment of Finland's political history.

8. R.J. Sontag and J.S. Beddie, (eds), *Nazi-Soviet Relations 1939-1951: Documents from the Archives of the German Foreign Office* (Washington: Department of State, 1948).

9. In the United States, France, and Germany, government papers have long been available about World War II but not in the Soviet Union. Military men through their memoirs have revealed something about Soviet decisions. *The Great Patriotic War of the Soviet Union 1941-1945,* published by the Ministry of Defense, reveals that the war plan for the

occupation of Finland, worked out by the Chief of the General Staff, Marshall Shaposhni-kov, was rejected by Stalin as exaggerating the defense capacity of the Finns. Stalin instead turned to Marshall Meretskov, Commander of the Leningrad Military District, and asked him to make a plan for "the defense of the Soviet border against a Finnish attack and work out a counter attack after a possible Finnish military provocation". O.V. Kuusinen was appointed by Stalin as Meretskov's advisor in questions concerning Finland. Max Jacobsen, "Vinterkriget: Vad tänkte Kreml?" *Svenska Dagbladet,* 13 February 1980.

10. The clash between Sandler and Wigforss in the Social-Democratic government over the Åland policy is described by Sandler's son, Professor Åke Sandler of California State University, Los Angeles, as a clash between ideologies. Sandler tried to neutralize the Nordic countries as a bloc and back up Finland in her negotiations with Russia. Wigforss, as a Marxist, thought that Stalin's Soviet Union was more peace-loving than Tsarist Russia. Åke Sandler, "Rickard Sandlers utrikespolitik i nytt ljus" *Svenska Dagbladet,* 15 March 1978. See also ÅS, *Political Aspects of Swedish Diplomacy During World War II* (Berkeley: University of California, 1950) and Wilhelm Carlgren, *Varken - eller: reflexioner kring Sveriges Ålandspolitik 1938-1939* (Stockholm: Norstedt, 1977).

11. The Soviet renunciation of the Porkala naval-military base may well have been calculated to offset the physchological effect of their not so voluntary renunciation of Port Arthur the same year. Adam B. Ulman, *Expansion and Coexistence: The History of Soviet Foreign Policy 1917-1967* (New York: Preager, 1968), p. 555.

12. Jonathan Kandell, "Living in the Soviet Shadow", *International Herald Tribune,* 18-19 August 1979.

13. The term was a slogan of Tsar Peter, who in 1703 established a Russian foothold on the Baltic with the founding of St. Petersburg in Ingria, which had been just taken from Sweden. Armies of labor were drafted to work in the swamps along the lower Neva under appalling conditions.

14. The Finns and Estonians called Sweden *Ruotsi.* All names are derived from Swedish *Roden,* the ancient name for the navy organization, which had its landbase in Roslagen. The small vessels of the time (7th century and later) were rowed more often than sailed and all terms quoted were derived from the verb row, Sw. *ro,* Old Norse *roa.* The Varangians (Greek and Arabic) or Varjags (Russian) got their name from *var* (oath). They were men tied by an oath to serve the captain of the ship. The Vikings were farmers turned seafarers and merchants. They had no kings and did not accept coins. Money was weighed on their scales as so much gold or silver. Sweden became a kingdom and − after the Viking era − used coins in the 11th century.

15. Among the Vikings, scholars were unknown. They left no written records, neither in Russia nor in Western Europe or North America. The only exception are the runestones, of which there are several hundreds in the Stockholm region which often tell about trips to Gardariki. But runestones are not a medium for longwinded chronicles. What we know about the Vikings in Russia has been culled from contemporary Greek and Arab accounts or from Russian chronicles written down a century or more after the events.

16. C. John Colombos, *The International Law of the Sea,* 6th ed, (London: Longmans, 1967), p. 216.

17. The World War I control over the approaches of the Black Sea was on the list of Russian war aims. The annexation by Russia of Constantinople and of the littoral of the Bosphorus, the Dardanelles, and the Sea of Marmara was agreed to by Britain and France in secret treaties of March/April 1915. However, the Russian high command was unable to provide the ships and men needed to reach this aim. The Gallipoli expeditionary army of British, Australian, and New Zealand troops in 1915-1916 made a fruitless attempt to take the straits. In June 1953, Moscow assured Turkey that it had abandoned its claims to some Turkish provinces bordering the Soviet Union and to military bases in the straites, thus ending a Moscow-Ankara cold war. *(The New York Times,* 11-14 June 1953).

18. With the break between Stalin and Hitler in 1941 and the German invasion, labels had to be found that avoided this confusion. "Nazi" Germany becam "Fascist" Germany.

19. The Ukrainians, Georgians, Armenians, and Azerbaijani Turks.

20. Russia was still on the Julian Calendar until 1918. According to the old calendar, the revolution occured in October; after the Gregorian calendar, in November. The Julian calendar had been adopted by Russia in 1699. Prior to that reform, time was reckoned from Creation and the calendar year began on 1 September..

21. During the Great Depression of the 1930s, which made possible the rapid rise to power of Adolf Hitler, some intellectuals began to doubt the future of the market economy. An interest in the alternative, the centrally planned economy, was created, not the least in the United States. The ideological confrontation between the two systems was stressed in both camps.

22. Sontag and Beddie, *Nazi-Soviet Relations.*

23. The strong Roman Catholic orientation of modern Poland was evident when the Bishop of Cracow, Cardinal Karol Wojtyla, was elected in 1978, the first non-Italian Pope in modern times, and called John Paul II.

24. Gdańsk remained a Polish city until 1793 when it became part of Prussia. As a Polish port it enjoyed a larger hinterland than any of the German ports on the Baltic.

25. Nationalism was much less potent in the 16th and 17th centuries than today, and it was customary to have foreign rulers on the throne, but nowhere was the practice more prevalent than in Poland.

26. Sigismund moved the Polish capital from Cracow to Warsaw. He also participated in the Russian power struggle. For a short time his son Wladyslaw was the Russian Tsar, but Sigismund himself aspired to the Russian throne, which led to conflict.

27. The prayer of Mickeiwicz was finally fullfilled: "Our Lord, provide us with general war for the liberation of the people".

28. Ivar Högbom in a paper on the geopolitical situation of Poland around 1930 makes the comment that Richard Coudenhove-Kalergi's Pan-Europa ideas met with great interest in Danzig, as evident by the local press and by exhibitions in the local bookstores. In areas where nationalities are juxtaposed, supranational solutions to conflicts become attractive.

Högbom adds that it was probably no coincidence that Esperanto as an idea was born in prewar Poland.

29. Leopold Unger, "When Poland Was Carved Up", *International Herald Tribune,* 18 September 1979.

30. The three Baltic countries, Finland, Russia, and Prussia, were named for another people than the one now living there. It is a linguistic curiosity, probably not known to the average person in these countries.

31. The medieval herring fisheries in the Sound, of great importance to the economy of Denmark and the Hanseatic League, never came back in modern history. However, several periods of flourishing herring fisheries were experienced further to the north off the coast of Gothenburg and Bohuslän. The waters off western Norway have been more normal spawning grounds for herring.

32. The world tonnage of steamships exceeded that of sail ships in 1897.

33. A ratio (length of coast through surface) has been calculated by the Geographer of the US Department of State as an indication of the importance of the sea in the life of 142 states of the world. The seven coastal countries on the Baltic ranked as follows: Denmark 12, (Norway 38), Sweden 50, Finland 58, the German Democratic Republic 63, the Federal Republic of Germany 71, the Soviet Union 82, and Poland 88. The Geographer, US Department of State, "Sovereignty of the Sea", *Geographic Bulletin*, No. 3, October 1969.

Chapter 4

1. Many accidents or near-accidents on this busy sea route have been ascribed to the use of dated charts, e.g., the collision on 31 October 1979, between a Soviet tanker and the Soviet Antarctic research vessel *Oleniok*, which caught fire. The *Oleniok* moved in the wrong lane at Sprogø.

2. "Den danske Lods" 1925 and later supplements.

3. *Route T, 17 meters Transitroute, Skagen - Gedser N.E.* (Copenhagen: Danish Administration of Navigation and Hydrography, 1976).

4. Phillip B. Moberg, "VLCCs and International Straits," *Marine Affairs Journal*, 1976:4.

5. To the protests of the Hansa, King Erik replied that he did no more than many "lesser Princes and Lords" did in their territories. Was this a reference to the Rhine Dues, claimed from the time of Charlemagne?

6. The most common non-littoral homeports of current coasters in the Baltic are Hamburg and several ports in the Bremen area of littoral West Germany.

7. The two countries "shared" the "Father of International Law", Hugo Grotius, who in 1609 had published his *Mare Liberum* (The Free Sea) in which he argued for the freedom of

the seas, supporting the right of the Dutch to sail to the Indies. Ten years later he received a life sentence for his involvement with the Remonstrants, the liberal sect of the Calvinist Church. Grotius escaped from prison and eventually went into the Swedish diplomatic service, becoming Swedish ambassador to France in 1634. He served in that position until 1645 when he died.

The best known work of Hugo Grotius, *De jure belli ac pacis* (On the Law of War and Peace) was published in 1625. His letters to Axel Oxenstierna, who, after the death of Gustavus Adolphus, led Swedish partiicipation in the Thirty Years War, were printed in the Correspondence of Oxenstierna (Vol. 2, 1889, and Vol. 4, 1891).

8.   G.F. de Martens, "La neutralisation de Danemark", *Revue des deux mondes*, 1903. p. 323.

9.   The Göta Canal has 58 locks and can accomodate vessels of 32 meters in length, seven meters in beam and 2.8 meters of draft. Maximum speed is 4.8 knots. Because of ice, the canal is closed four months a year for repairs. It is now primarily used by pleasure boats, which accounted for over 90% of the revenue in 1977 but only 15% in 1960 when cargo vessels still provided 75%. Gert Åkesson, *Göta Kanal* (Malmö: Stenwall, 1979).

10.   Quote from Brüel, p. 37, who quotes an American note to Copenhagen 1848, which drew on Henry Wheaton, *A History of the Law of Nations* (1845).

11.   Erik Brüel, *International Straits* (Copenhagen: Busck - London: Sweet & Maxwell, 1947), pp. 55-56.

12.   Edward Crankshaw, *The Shadow of the Winter Palace* (New York: Viking, 1976), p. 136.

13.   W.R. Mead and S.H. Jaatinen, *The Åland Islands* (London: David and Charles, 1974), p. 97.

14.   Goethe's views on laws and lawyers may also apply to military strategists: *"Es erben sich Gesetz und Rechte ... sie schleppen vom Geschlecht sich zum Geschlechte"*. That the arguments of international lawyers and strategists about the Baltic Straits have a familiar ring through the centuries should be obvious from this book.

15.   When Sweden in 1658 became a littoral state on the Sound the Danish King claimed sovereignty over the whole strait. Territorial waters were still an unknown concept. After 1779 Sweden claimed four miles. See T. Gihl, *Gränsen för Sveriges Territorialvatten*, 1930). The Danish claim was three miles, except in the Sound where it was four. Sweden claimed the mid-line where the Sound was less than eight miles wide but Denmark claimed the mid-line in Flintrännan. The border between the two countries became Flintrännan during World War I when half the channel was Danish and half Swedish, but in 1932 an agreement was reached in which Flintrännan was placed completely within Swedish jurisdiction.

By the Treaty of Frederiksborg (1720), Sweden, in exchange for the return of the territory conquered by Denmark during the war gave up its ancient freedom from tolls in the Sound. However, in 1839-1840 there was a sharp exchange of views between Sweden and Denmark, with Stockholm maintaining that it was "unheard of" for a country to pay dues on shipping along its own coast. Denmark replied that this was in return for the conquered territories restored in 1720 (Brüel, pp. 35-36).

16. Winston Churchill, *The World Crisis 1914-1916*. Part II (London: Scribner 1927), pp. 640 ff.

17. Brüel, p. 76.

18. Oppenheim, pp. 482-483.

19. Sikkerhedspolitisk studiegruppe, *Østersøen: Geografi, Historie, Økonomi, Havret, Forsvar, Sikkerhed* (Copenhagen: Schultz, 1979).

20. See e.g., Edward Wegener, "Die Seegebiete: Nordflanke der NATO und Nordatlantic" in D. Mahncke & H-P Schwarz, *Seemacht und Aussenpolitik* (Frankfurt aM: Metzner, 1974), p. 301.

21. Under NATO's Supreme Command in Europe (SHAPE), headquartered at Casteau, Belgium, are three regional commands, of which Command North (AFNORTH) at Kolsås, Norway comprises Norway, Denmark, Schleswig-Holstein, and the Baltic Approaches. COMBALTAP is the southern command under AFNORTH.

22. Christopher von Schirach-Szmigiel, *Liner Shipping and General Cargo Transport* (Stockholm: EFI, 1979), p. 177.

23. Eugene Kozicharow, "Soviet Buildup in Baltic Troubles Danes," *Aviation Week & Space Technology,* 13 November 1978, pp. 49-55 and Horst von Schroeder, "The Allied Command Naval Forces Baltic Approaches", *NATO's Fifteen Nations Special 1978,* pp. 36-39.

24. The requirement that submarines surface when transiting straits should be of little interest to the major naval powers who have sophisticated detection systems and for whom submerged passage is equally obvious as surface passage. Fredric G. De Rocher, *Freedom of Passage Through International Straits: Community Interest Amid Present Controversy* (Coral Gables, Fla.: Sea Grant Program, University of Florida, 1972), Technical Bulletin No. 23, pp. 27 ff. The US Navy can identify WP submarines by their motor sounds as each individual vessel makes its own individual noise, which can be instantly identified by a computer. The equipment of the three Soviet signal vessels stationed at the entrance of the Baltic since the early 1970s and of the one in the Strait of Hormuz on duty since the fall of 1979 are not known in detail but should be quite sophisticated.

25. Information taken for granted in the "open countries" of the West (statistics on port traffic, production of various metals etc.) are state secrets in the Soviet Union.

26. Robert E. Osgood, "US Security Interests and the Law of the Sea," in Ryan C. Amacher and Richard J. Sweeney, eds., *The Law of the Sea: US Interests and Alternatives* (Washington, D.C.: American Enterprise Institute for Public Policy Research, 1976), p. 13.

27. *Völkerrecht - Lehrbuch, Teil I* (Berlin: Staatsverlag der DDR, 1973), p. 387.

28. P.D. Barabolia ed., *Voenno-morskoj mezdunarodno-pravovoj spravocnik, (Moscow, 1966)*, p. 170-171. Also *Völkerecht - Lehrbuch*, p. 386.

29. The two ordinances repealed respectively the Danish ordinance of 25 July 1951 and the Swedish ordinance of 8 June 1951. The English texts of the two ordinances have been appended before these notes.

30. The treaty of 1857 did not establish a special regime for the Baltic Straits. It only removed a hindrance to shipping. Brüel, Vol. II, pp. 40 and 58 and Ruth Lapidoth, *Les détroits en droits international* (Paris: Pendone, 1972), p. 112.

31. The debate on bill 1979/80:16 by the Foreign Relations Committee, *The Quick Records of the Riksdag,* Friday 18 December 1979, Georg Åberg, Liberal, Speech 28, pp. 46-49.

32. How much this would interfere with their work cannot be judged by a layman. The absence of NATO patrol boats outside the 12-mile territorial sea near Leningrad could be interpreted as an indication that the desired information cannot be obtained from a vessel at such distance from the coast or that it can be better received from airplanes.

33. Jan Bergqvist, Speech 27, pp. 41-46, and Birger Rosqvist, Speech 29, *The Quick Records of the Riksdag,* pp. 49-50. Both men were Social Democrats.

34. J. Haalck & G. Reintanz, *Internationales Seerecht* (Leipzig, 1973), p. 61.

35. Renate Platzöder, *Völkerrechtliche und politische auswirkungen der dritten Seerechtskonferenz der Vereinten Nationen auf Nord- und Ostsee* (Ebenhausen bei München: Stiftung Wissenschaft und Politik, 1978), p. 50.

36. Platzöder, p. 52.

37. G. Alexandersson and G. Norström, *World Shipping* (Stockholm: Almqvist and Wiksell - New York: Wiley, 1963), pp. 224-225.

38. Brüel, pp. 42-44.

39. Landfills occur in all harbors along the three straits and sand dredging takes place in many spots. They influence the profiles of the straits in opposite ways but so far only on a submarginal scale. Actions that lower the turnover time of the water and increase the salt content should benefit the living resources of the Baltic Sea and vice versa. Dredging should thus be preferred to landfilling and damming.

40. The closed sea doctrine was the rule in the 17th century and earlier.

41. The German phrase "der petrinische Anspruch" summarizes the Russian policy in the Baltic since the days of Tsar Peter the Great. Edward Wegener, op. cit., p. 299.

42. B.A. Dranov, *Chernomorskie prolivy: mezhdunarodno-pravovoi rezhim* (Moscow: Jurizdat, 1948). S.V. Molodtsov: 'Mezhdunarodno-pravovoi rezhim baltiishih prolivov' *SGIP,* no. 5 (1950). For a Western comment to the study of Dranov couched in Cold War terms, see K. Grzybowski, "The Soviet Doctrine of Mare Clausum and Policies in Black and Baltic Seas", *Journal of Central European Affairs,* 1954-55, Vol. 14, pp. 339-353.

43. L. Oppenheim, *International Law*, Vol. 1, 8th ed., L. Lauterpacht, editor (London: Longman, 1955), p. 97.

44. Oppenheim, p. 588.

45. J.G. Starke, *An Introduction to International Law* (5th ed.), 1963, and Article III of the Geneva Convention of the High Seas.

46. France de Hartingh, *Les conceptions soviétiques du droit de la mer* (Paris: Pichon & Durand-Auzias, 1960), p. 28.

47. Toivo Miljan, "Mare Clausum Balticum and the Law of the Sea", *Osteuropa Recht,* Vol. 21, Nr. 2, 1975, p. 111.

48. Platzöder, p. 125.

49. Platzöder, p. 127.

50. The omission of the standard 'closed sea' formulation and an abbreviated list of 'historic waters' in a Soviet treatise of 1969 is interpreted by Butler as an indication that both doctrines may be in disrepute in some quarters of the Soviet legal establishment. William E. Butler, *The Soviet Union and the Law of the Sea* (Baltimore: John Hopkins, 1971).

Chapter 5

1. The following pages summarize a paper by Bernt I. Dybern, "The Organizational Pattern of Baltic Marine Science" in a special issue of *Ambio,* 1980:3-4, published by the Royal Swedish Academy of Sciences, devoted to various aspects of the Baltic Sea.

2. Carl Björeman, "Ockupation av Sydsverige". *Sydsvenska Dagbladet Snällposten,* 28 February, 1981. Björeman, who is chief-of-staff, Military District South, lists the large Warsaw Pact naval units in the Baltic as four cruisers, 50 destroyers and frigates, six nuclear missile carrying submarines and 55 other submarines.

INDEX

128